Like Ripples in a Pond

Karen Destun

Foreword by Mark Hamilton,
The Olive Reader

Like Ripples in a Pond
Copyright © 2023 Karen Destun
ISBN: 978-1-990330-37-7

Editing and formatting: Lisa Browning
One Thousand Trees - www.onethousandtrees.com

*This book is dedicated to the children
who have died before their time, and the parents
and families who feel the grief and pain of that loss.*

*"Grief, I've learned, is really just love.
It's all the love you want to give, but cannot.
All that unspent love gathers up in the corners of your eyes,
the lump in your throat, and in that hollow part of your chest.
Grief is just love with no place to go."*

~Jamie Anderson

TABLE OF CONTENTS

Foreword

This book is a deep reading book that looks at the joys and sadness, the highs and lows of life. By getting to know Karen and some of her family, this book will touch your heart about Lauren, and the joy she brought to many people. This includes people that never met her in this realm.

As a medium I have dealt with death for years, and in doing this I asked Lauren to share her thoughts from Heaven. This may be strange to many but she always wants to help.

Lauren said, *Always remember to live as if it's your last days, as you never know when they may be. Enjoy the moments of just being; even a bad day brings learning and joy. I filled so much into my life, that I really can't complain. I lived as I wished and was loved by so many. I may have had a short life but it was filled with so much. I had joy, happiness, and sadness, but no regrets as I had my people.*

This book takes you on a journey of pain, but also a journey of remembering the joy of Lauren. It also shows the strength of Karen. This book will help others by reminding them that they are not alone in their own journey of grief. Pain is different for everyone. Karen has done so much in helping other bereaved parents since the loss of Lauren, and continues shining a beacon of light to those who can't see it at this moment.

This book is a powerful and hard reminder of the difficulties of life, but also the joys.

Take that moment — each moment — hold what's important and let go of things that are not serving your highest good.

Fly high, Lauren; thank you for being you, and for the light you brought to this world.

Mark Hamilton
The Olive Reader

Preface

The following writing has been in my mind, in notes on my phone, posts on facebook, notes written on a steno pad while sitting in hospital rooms, scribbles in a year's agenda book, and in my heart.

Life experiences. Moments in time that shape us. Really all I wanted was an ordinary life, but life had a different plan.

Prologue

Most days are like any other; the busyness of life takes over. Some days I go through the motions, occupied with the things that seem to float me through each day on a wave of constant activity. Other days it all hits me like a brick. I sit stunned, trying to figure out what hit me and why.

A friend said to me, "… you are all as tough as nails." And I thought to myself, but nails will bend.

A carpenter bends nails to anchor and strengthen. This ensures that an important part of a structure cannot be destroyed.

Late Spring 1999

The rain has started. I can see it as I look out of our kitchen window. There is a beautiful difference between a cold autumn rain, and a warm spring or summer one. Theo is sitting at my feet as I finish up the dishes. It's coming down pretty hard, but the air is warm and the smell of the earth and fresh grass is so inviting.

I lean down to pick up my bright-eyed baby and hitch him to my hip. "Let's go," I say. "We're going to run in the rain." I swing open the door and run down the backyard path. Theo giggles and holds tight as I open the gate and begin to run down the sidewalk that is now filling with puddles of freshly fallen rain. He clings to me, his arms around my neck, his small warm head nestled at my neck as my arms wrap around him. I run a few houses down the street, turn and run back to the corner. I hear Theo laughing and feel him bouncing against me. We run again, water splashing as my bare feet hit the sidewalk, rain still falling.

* * *

Fondly remember sitting on my front porch during a summer rain and watching Karen with Lauren in arms. Barefoot running in the rain. Stanley Street was full of joy when you saw Karen and her children laughing and running in the rain.

Bev Widmeyer

Diagnosis 2016

It was an assault. The sounds, the smells, what we saw. We had walked off the elevator and kept to the left as we were told. "3F Clinic is off the elevator… go left, and we're on the right. Go up to the cubicle and talk to the woman in the last window." We hadn't been told the name of the clinic, so when we saw the sign, my heart stopped. *Oncology and Haematology.* This was a waiting room and clinic all in one. Doors to private exam rooms lined either side of the rectangular room. The clinic was packed full of people. Nurses moving swiftly through the pockets of families. Children of many ages, adults dutifully with them. How could it be that this many kids needed to be at this clinic? We are here for tests. Tests. What kinds of tests? What would they tell us?

* * *

Less than a month earlier, strange symptoms had started to emerge. Aches and pains that were often dismissed as there was what seemed to be a legitimate reason for them. A sore shoulder was the first. It seemed to coincide with a trip to the sliding hill which could explain the pain. A trip to the ER where an x-ray was done showed no indication of injury. Given the pain, a second x-ray was done to be sure that there was not an issue with the growth plate. Within a week, the shoulder pain had subsided but now we were dealing with a sore foot.

Once again, x-rays didn't show any injury, and a parachute game with friends seemed to be a good explanation for a minor injury. Soon the foot healed, but wrist pain now took over. These aches and pains were accompanied by inability to move the offended joint. Once again, investigations included examinations, x-rays and now blood work that would come back showing nothing. As these symptoms showed from one joint to the other, a strange swelling on the face was becoming cause for concern. It was this swelling, along with the wrist pain, that would lead us to our visit to the Oncology and Haematology Clinic at McMaster Children's Hospital. Our paediatrician initially concluded that the swelling was a dental problem and she suggested that a dentist should be consulted. After she questioned whether the wrist pain and face swelling along with the previous foot pain, and shoulder pain were related, we were sent home. The next day a phone call from her office directed us to an ultrasound and CT scan. The results of these tests were to be sent to McMaster, and they would hopefully have answers.

Did we want these answers? It was all such a whirlwind. In the meantime, I took a couple of days off from my regular routine, and we stayed home . We spent time doing some fun activities while we silently wondered what was unfolding before us. I remember feeling as though control of our lives was being ripped from our grasp.

* * *

We stood in the clinic room. We were in shock. We listened and watched as, around us, so many families sat, or stood with their children. Some children were obviously in the midst of cancer treatments. Their bald heads stark contrast to the hair that should have been there. Their pale and often chubby faces sometimes smiling, often in a state of fatigue, eyes closed as they curled up in the lounge chairs provided for children with IV poles dangling their treatments. The room was warm, and noisy. There were few seats to be found. Amidst the din of conversation, the noise of the place was irritating, as it clashed between laughter and IV machines beeping. Nurses bobbed about, speaking with children and families, taking heights and weights, directing the next in line to examination rooms.

We were called into an exam room, furnished with a few chairs, a patient examination table, and a toddler table and chairs. The room and lights were bright. The walls donned a few medical posters, as well as the typical collection of medical paraphernalia. We sat nervously, trying to make light of what increasingly seemed like a nightmare. We were met by a nurse practitioner who took a lengthy history from us. This would be the first of many times the story of aches and pains would be relayed. Our beautiful child remained stoic throughout, showing a brave and courageous front. While this scenario was different, it held a pang of the familiar. I felt we were on the edge of a precipice that we had walked before.

Part 1

Building a Family

The One - 1991

A mutual friend or family member suggests that these two people would be great together. I hadn't been seeing anyone. By the age of 26 I had been in a couple of relationships, one that had brought me to Ontario from Nova Scotia. When a co-worker introduced me to her cousin Mike, I was intrigued. His smile was enchanting and he was a musician. Growing up, music had always been a large part of my life, so this was attractive to me. We had a connection that we wanted to pursue. After a few movie dates, it seemed we were hooked. Mike was going to York University at the time, as well as playing with a band that travelled. While a lot of those early days were spent apart, a love for each other was beginning to grow.

As our relationship blossomed, it seemed only natural that I should take Mike to meet my family. This would not be as easy as asking my mom to invite him to dinner. Being a few provinces away from my hometown, we would have to make a cross-country trip to introduce him to my mom and my sisters. We decided to take a camping trip east. Mike was slightly annoyed that I was trying to 'plan his life.' He intimated that by thinking ahead about when we should go and making lists I was taking away his spontaneity. Later I learned it might be one of my traits that he was grateful for. We packed his truck and headed east with a borrowed tent. Despite my urging, he insisted that we did not need much more. We had a map and a plan.

* * *

Camping has always been a part of my life. As long as I can remember, our family went camping. I eagerly took on the job of trip navigator. In the 70s, this title afforded the keeper of the map a front seat spot in the big Chevy sedan that Dad drove. We would make trips to Prince Edward Island, New Brunswick, and sometimes down into the New England States, adventuring into beautiful seaside spots, natural wooded areas and small towns. Each night we would stop at a campground, set up, cook supper and enjoy some time by the fire. For my sister Heather and me, finding a spot that had a lake or a pool was exciting. A tour through the campground would give us a quick glimpse into how far we'd have to walk to get to the playground or a place to swim.

* * *

I was ready for this! Camping as an adult was going to be a breeze. I had trained for it my whole life. I had bought and packed some of the foods I remembered enjoying as a kid on our camping trips. Little did I know that Mike thought it a huge joke, and had unpacked some of these things. Funny guy!

On our first night, we stopped at Alexandria Bay on the St. Lawrence River, just across the border into New York State. It was a beautiful spot. We set up what little we had for camping gear and as the sun set, and our fire burned, we realized we didn't have any form of lighting. We stumbled through this first night, and were back on the road the next day. When we found ourselves in a small New York town, we went to the first store we could find that had camping supplies. We purchased a couple of flashlights, our first camp stove, and a propane lantern. I was excited to be taking this trip back to my home, through areas that I remembered as a child. Our yearly camping trips to New England offered wonderful memories.

If this trip was to be a test of our relationship, then hail to the teacher! We weren't long on the highway heading south before making an abrupt turn to head east towards Vermont. We had heard on the radio that there might be stormy skies overnight. It was August, and it was hurricane season in the Atlantic, so anything was possible. Weather reports were indicating a storm coming up the coast. It seemed hurricane Bob was on its way. We found a campground in the Green Mountains for the night, where we were surrounded by the beauty of the landscape, and loving it! We set up camp, made some supper and settled in. It rained through the night, but things were dry by the morning. We were pleased to be back on the road by late morning. The scenic drive through Vermont and New Hampshire was incredible. I was navigating our trip through dotted towns and villages that I remembered visiting during family vacations as a child. When we got into Maine we decided to drive towards the coast, and track the seaside towns. Up to this point, we had paid no more than $7 a night for campsites. A nightly rate of $25 at a "Camping Resort" seemed as though we were splurging. It seemed it would be worthwhile, with a shuttle bus to the lobster hut as well as a host of local activities. Being close to the ocean again was good for my soul. It was late afternoon, and it had been a gorgeous sunny day for travelling, and sightseeing. We began to pull out our camp gear and prepare for a relaxing night. We thought we might take a shuttle to the beach town to wander the streets. As we cooked some supper, the clouds rolled in, and without warning, the sky opened up like an endless waterfall. We could feel in that moment that this rain was not going to pass through quickly. It was here to stay. The wind was picking up, and we were forced to make some quick decisions. We pulled all of the bedding out of the tent and threw it in the back of the Ford Ranger. The coolers were pulled into the tent and our luggage was piled on top to hopefully avoid our clothing getting soaked from the streams of water now flowing through the tent. In the pouring rain, we put away as much as we could, sometimes storing things under the truck or the picnic table, before climbing into the back of the truck. The truck bed was just big enough for the two of us to fit lying down. In the jumble of sleeping bags and mattresses we struggled to lay everything out, knowing we'd be in for a long night. The rain didn't falter at all. There were a couple of corners of the truck where water would drip in. Much to our annoyance, a number of mosquitos were enjoying the dry space with us. Armed with a flashlight and a wadded up sock, we spent the night reducing these little winged whiners to spider food. The daddy long legs that had taken up webbed residence in the corner of the truck was thrilled, I'm sure.

By early morning we were exhausted, soggy, and thoroughly annoyed. The Camping Resort looked a mess with downed branches and leaves everywhere. All we could do was pack up and get back on the road. From our mad dash the night before in the pouring rain, our shoes were soaked. We started back on the road in silence, both of us needing a good dry rest. We hadn't really eaten a good supper the night before, so we decided to stop at a Dunkin' Donuts for coffee and some food. In our reduced state of reasoning, this led to our first argument. Mike suggested that we get a dozen donuts for the road. I made it clear that I didn't think donuts were the right choice for an early morning meal and suggested that muffins would be a better choice. Neither of us would change our minds, nor did either of us realize until years later that a compromise of 6 of one, ½ a dozen of the other might work. To this day, we laugh over this memory. For the remainder of the day, we silently stewed over donuts and muffins while our feet squished in wet shoes.

We had coffee and nothing to eat, and we were back on the road. After travelling further up the coast of Maine, we eventually made it to Ellsworth. Here we did some shopping for food, some dry shoes, and some more supplies. We decided to stay in the area for the night, and did some visiting with family who were cottaging in Trenton. We took in some of the sites around Mount Pleasant Island and Bar Harbor. That night we rented a cabin, in search of a good dry rest. We ordered steamed clams from a local lobster pound for supper, and I taught Mike the art of gorging on seafood.

Within a couple of days, we arrived in Nova Scotia. I can't remember how long it had been since I had been home. This was definitely the first time I was bringing someone to my mom's from Ontario. I was enjoying showing Mike all the things I loved about Truro, and all of Nova Scotia. If we could survive a camping trip across provinces and states, a hurricane, and a deal breaker argument about coffee shop pastries, surely our relationship could handle anything.

During a summer tour on the road, Mike travelled with the band True Blue, to Northern Ontario and points west. Neither of us had email. Cell phones were not a common thing, so we wrote letters. Perhaps it is more accurate to say I wrote letters. Mike would call me after he received one. It seemed a long time to be apart, and I took a chance. I knew the tour schedule and decided to drive to Kapuskasing to the bar they would be playing as they made their way back from Manitoba and once again into Northern Ontario. I drove the many hours from St. Thomas to Timmins. I guess I did it in one day. At that age, those ten hours in the car, driving roads I had never been on, was exciting. I found a motel room for a couple of nights, and rested for a while before making the trip to Kapuskasing, another couple of hours north. There wasn't really much to the town of Kapuskasing, and finding the bar where True Blue was playing was easy. I stepped in, and found a table. I'm sure it was a surprise for Mike to see me there. We drove back to Timmins together that night, and I stayed a few more days as they continued this leg of their tour at the Maple Leaf in Timmins. Mike's dad had grown up in that area. It was wonderful to meet Mike's grandparents and some of his aunts and uncles. I was beginning to feel that this was more than just a casual relationship. He could be the one.

One night, Mike came in from outside, beckoning me to follow him back out. He motioned upwards and I tilted my head to see an incredible light show. We walked until we were past the lights of the town. Lying on our backs on the golf course, away from manmade lights, the sky was a stunning glow of magical hues. Looking up at this night sky, I felt I could take anything on. The possibilities of our future were vast and bright, shining and flowing like the iridescent brilliance of the aurora borealis.

Mike drove back to Southern Ontario with me, and not much longer after that, anytime he came home from university, it would be to my apartment in St. Thomas. Eventually we knew that, together, we wanted to build a life. We moved from St. Thomas to Waterloo Region. Our lives were full of the promise of young love, work and dreams. Mike continued to play in a band as well as teach drums. I had transitioned from working in St. Thomas and Guelph simultaneously, to working in Hamilton. Living in Kitchener seemed less central to what we needed, and Cambridge became an attractive option. It was after our move to this small city that our dreams of making a promise to each other happened.

The band that Mike was working with at the time had many followers who were good friends. People who they had known over the years through school and family connections. Peggy was one of those people. We soon formed a friendship, and spent many evenings together enjoying the music that brought us together. It is hard not to smile when reminiscing about some of the things that happened in those early days. I'm sure Peggy would laugh, recalling how we drove through a snowstorm from the border of Ontario and Michigan to Dundas just to sit in the Owl's Roost to hear a song or two. We white-knuckled the drive back to Paris Ontario with hopes of getting a decent sleep, only to be awakened the following morning by the crash of cymbals as the town's annual Christmas Parade filled the streets whilst playing The Nutcracker Suite.

After a few years, we were planning our wedding. With much help from family and friends, our small backyard wedding happened on an overcast summer evening in August, 1996. Young and in love, we were taking on the world. Our world.

* * *

Quiet November Morning - 1998

The two of us together were a family in the little starter home that we had bought. We were busy, with Mike drumming and teaching, and me working in mail distribution. Life was good, and we were happy. We had a couple of dogs, and cats, and I would often walk our dogs down at the park just a block from our home. One evening I met a fellow who was at the park running his dog as well. We chatted, and he told me his spouse would likely love to meet me as they had recently moved in around the corner. Turns out her name was also Karen, and we became fast friends. Karen and I would meet to walk our dogs, often taking them to a local tract of land used for hiking. The dogs would run and socialize. Karen and I would talk. We had a strong kinship, the kind where you felt you could fix world problems if only people would listen, or write books about trees and plants found along the hiking trail. These walks and talks meant the world to me. I felt connected to the earth.

After a few years, Mike and I were ready to create some little ones. Our desire to add to our family was happening. Before long, our days were full of anticipation of our new addition. We would soon be welcoming a little being. While I was pregnant, we continued to enjoy camping, and our growing circle of friends. I walked the trails with the dogs nearly every day, until I went into labour.

Within a few months of my becoming pregnant, Karen was also expecting. It was amazing to have a friend to go through pregnancy with. Our daily walks and talks on the trails were full of conversations about babies, pregnancy, and parenting. We were sure we would be able to write a book about these topics as well, as we endeavoured to learn all we could about our changing roles and responsibilities.

As do most newly pregnant couples, we took a prenatal class. Mike and I dutifully went to all classes, and inevitably bonded with the other couples over our shared situations. Our instructor set a date for a reunion, which would be at least a month following all of our due dates.

I had been working as an office temp at a trucking company in Ayr. My last day was on a Friday, a week before the baby's due date, and I was looking forward to a week at home, preparing for our son or daughter. We had decided to have a home birth, attended by a midwife. I was anticipating that I would go late, as was usual with first-time pregnancies. On Monday, November 23rd, after Mike had left for work, I realized that we were out of toilet paper. We were a one-car family, and Mike had taken the car to work, so my need for paper products would have to be filled by a walk up the hill to the local Biway store. I had done so much walking throughout my pregnancy, that surely a short walk up the hill and back wouldn't be a problem. By the time I got home, without toilet paper I might add, the dull ache in my lower back was becoming more acute. The strangest things can stay with you. I was so surprised that a store like Biway didn't carry toilet paper. I'm sure Mike arrived home from work much later with a fresh stock, and excited concern. By this time, it was clear that I was in labour. However, I was not at all prepared for the back pain that seemed to accompany each contraction. I tried sitting, and often sprawling my body across the birthing ball that we had purchased. No amount of rocking on this rubber sphere would alleviate the pressure in my lower back. We had prepared a sock stuffed with rice, to be heated and used to ease any contraction pain. I'm sure Mike still remembers the insistence with which I pleaded that he push harder on my back with this rice roll, to no avail.

Our midwife, Nadine, had been contacted. Our bedroom was prepared according to the birthing plan that had been devised weeks before, ensuring safety and comfort. I laboured into the night, taking each contraction and its painful twisting of my lower back. Nadine diligently checking the baby's heart rate, and my dilation. After a few hours, there was a small cause for concern. The heart rate of the baby was taking a dip with the contractions, lower than was safe. As with protocol for a home birth, we opted to go to the hospital to be sure that the baby and I would be fine as we continued with our labour. It was a cold dark night. Clear and calm. Sitting in the car was not at all comfortable. The short drive to the hospital felt like an hour.

Once in the hospital, it wasn't long before we had a room and I was able to rest my back. A few small checks showed that the baby was fine. I laboured through the night, feeling exhausted and ready to be done by morning. Soon the back pain subsided, and I was ready to push. This was the easy part. Mike might disagree, having of course never witnessed a birth before, let alone the birth of his first son. Theodore James came into our lives on this quiet, sunny November morning, three days early. Despite the back pain, it was a beautiful experience. Theo was a happy, healthy baby, and we were thrilled. He was pure joy. The early days were filled with the usual chores of having an infant. We were exhausted, in shock, and ecstatic with love for this little being.

Only a few weeks after he was born, I noticed that Theo seemed slightly congested. I was concerned about this sweet little boy and, being a new mother, I didn't want to take any chances. The more I observed, the more obvious it was that he was struggling to breathe. I whisked him out to the hospital emergency room, hoping that I was being overly cautious. It turned out that I had good motherly instincts.

He had a respiratory virus, a cold, but for one so young, it was too much for his little system to handle. We stayed in the paediatric ward for a couple of nights, while Theo was observed for improvement, getting ventolin treatments to help open his airway. That was our first experience with a sick child admitted to the hospital. It was not one that I wanted to repeat.

There had been a reunion scheduled with the other couples and new babies from our prenatal group, coincidentally the day Theo was discharged from the hospital. We literally went from his room down the hall to a meeting room where we were to connect with these families. I was so incredibly nervous that we would inadvertently pass any remnant of the cold that Theo had on to one of the other infants. I didn't want any of the other infants to end up hospitalized because of us. My sharp instinct was to watch hawk-like, ensuring that no one came within a few feet of us. I was sure that if another parent touched him, the germs of the cold would then be transmitted to their child. I was completely terrified. I'm sure it was slightly confusing to the other parents as there was little time to explain. The chances were so slim. We were overly cautious, and it showed. I may have made a few of the other new parents slightly nervous with my insistence to be aware of germs. Regardless, we enjoyed this little reconnection to these new families. Our prenatal instructor said she had never taught a group that was so connected. We all decided to meet again in roughly six months to catch up. It was a fun and hopeful time in our lives. We enjoyed the company of these couples; however, one family would remain a constant in our lives for many years.

Dagmar and Russell lived just outside of Cambridge. They were in many ways different from us, originally from out west, both from farming families. They had lived in Toronto prior to moving to

Waterloo Region. Russell was a pilot, Dagmar an aspiring English professor. Our boys were born within a week of one another. Following our connection through the prenatal group, we began visiting one another so that the boys could play, and the adults could chat. A friendship was forged. When Theo and Rob were about six months old, Dagmar and Russell asked if I would be interested in helping them by looking after Rob a few hours a week while Dagmar worked on her thesis. This was my first taste at providing childcare. Rob and Theo didn't see each other often, but when they did, they were always fast friends.

As Theo grew and learned, I enjoyed motherhood immensely, wanting to soak up every moment, and learn with him. I felt it important that I keep him close, so I chose to use a sling to carry him in. I was pleased that I was able to breastfeed. It was a wonderful bonding. It was important to me that I nurse my babies as long as possible. I was still breastfeeding Theo right up until our second was born. Theo went everywhere I did, in the sling, even on forest walks with our dogs. His first playmate was Rob, as they had known each other since Dagmar and I sat with swollen baby bellies in prenatal class.

After Karen had Nathan, he and Theo became friends. The boys were now part of our daily trail walks with the dogs, often snuggled in their slings sleeping while we traversed the hills and valleys of the tract.

By some standards, we were sheltered. My full-time work was being a mom, so Theo was with me all day every day. Our extended family was not close by, so we didn't have convenient sitters. I was fine with the way things were.

I remember taking Theo to a playground for the first time. He was just over a year old. With trepidation I helped him to climb the ladder stairs up and into the play structure. At that point, I had relinquished control to him. I couldn't climb up and hold his hand, I couldn't physically direct his travel. Suddenly I had left it up to him. It felt terrifying. I was also weighed with the complete understanding of my role as his mother. To prepare him for this world. To teach him, and learn that he is a part of something bigger. To teach him kindness, gentleness, and responsibility.

Theo slept, smiled, babbled, crawled, and walked into toddler-hood. When time allowed, we began to dream about a brother or sister for him. Soon Dagmar and I were both expecting again, and the timing was similar. Our due dates were in October of 2000.

That summer, we drove to Elora Gorge to enjoy the campground there. Dagmar, Russel and Rob joined us for dinner one night. We laughed and talked about life in general, fully taking in the joy of being families and friends. As our families were growing, we hoped the connection would continue.

A Sibling - 2000

We have always gotten by. Sometimes just by the edge of our teeth. We have managed over the years, and done our best to provide as we should for our family. Any dreams of travelling were often curtailed due to finances and worry over health issues. I often look back, and do wish we'd been able to travel as a family out of province more often. Specifically, I would have liked to visit with my family more frequently. Strange to realize, but our family in its entirety was never able to travel together to see my home in Nova Scotia. Mike and I travelled there a couple of times before we were married. The trip for our wedding was amazing, as we travelled with Mike's brother and his wife through New England, camping along the way. Following our wedding, we camped through Cape Breton before making the trip back to Ontario. When Theo was not quite two, the two of us flew to Nova Scotia to visit. I was seven months pregnant with Zach at the time, with no inkling of how our life would change after his birth.

By all accounts, all went well with my second pregnancy. Going back to our previous midwife was top of the list. We were happy to have Nadine with us again, and all appointments seemed to be textbook for a healthy pregnancy and healthy baby. Each check and measurement was in line. Theo was getting excited to welcome a new brother or sister into our lives. Again, we planned a home birth. Our bedroom was set up and ready to welcome this growing bundle of love.

The due date was October 20th. I wasn't sure what to expect, with Theo having been early. I supposed in those late days of the forty weeks, that early would be so wonderful. I planned for it. Expected a similar experience. My mind would skip over the birth part, and get caught up in the anticipation of the first hours and days of having a newborn beside me. I dreamed about the love and comfort of my little family as we would navigate those sleepy days with a new baby. Throughout the pregnancy, I would often have flashes of what I can only call intuition now. I was getting a sense that something was wrong. For some reason, these feelings would often be accompanied by the thought that it was something oral, sometimes something more. But all medical indications throughout pointed to a healthy baby. I put aside my fears as being misplaced worry.

When ten days after the due date had passed, I was more than ready. For the first time since we had been together, Mike and I had the Halloween treats ready for the night of the thirty-first. On October 30th, I went into labour. I remember sunshine. I sat at our dining table eating soup. I walked through our tiny house when I needed to. Back labour was constant again. I was determined that we would do this at home, but also knew that if we had to, we would go to the hospital as we had done when Theo was born. Nadine checked the baby's heart rate and my dilation progress, and things were going well. After a few hours, however, my condition was unsettling. I felt as though I was turning inward with each contraction, as though every cell in my body was leaking energy. I just wanted to lie in a curled up ball. The baby's heart rate was now dipping concerningly low with the contractions. The blur of energy around me now was muffled and peaked. The day was cold, with the stretcher blanket barely able to keep the wind from chilling me. Being lifted into the back of the ambulance, I recall saying that I just wanted to sleep. That's all, just sleep and I'd be fine.

I suppose Mike and Nadine were there when I arrived at the hospital. I told a nurse that I felt like pushing. She screamed at me.

Don't do that! I was annoyed. I just needed to voice how I felt. There were hands, and faces all around me, manoeuvring my body into a position that was so against what my body wanted. I heard the word forceps, and felt the hard pull as this our new little boy was brought into the world. I don't even remember if he was placed on my chest. I just knew I was tired, and this is not how I'd wanted things to go. Out of my control. But he was here, and I hoped healthy. Sleep, dazed sleep, and then please just can we go home?

It was a time when we should have been revelling in the birth of our baby boy, but instead, we were faced with the grim reality that he might die. The birth of our second child took a turn when the fetal heart rate indicated distress, and my ability to cope indicated maternal stress. A very quick forceps delivery was performed and baby Zachary Quin was whisked away. He seemed to be having trouble breathing. He was placed in an incubator providing him with 100% oxygen. Over time, he seemed to be doing well, and it was expected that I would be able to take him home the next day. I just wanted to take my baby home to be with my husband and son. I didn't want either of us to have to spend time in the hospital.

My sister Linda and her husband Barry had arrived from Nova Scotia a few days ahead of my going into labour, and we were so happy to have them there to help. They stayed and cared for Theo during labour and Zach's birth, and were excited to see us home soon. Following Zach's birth, they visited the hospital, and Barry took the first photo of Zach. He looked so beautiful. I couldn't wait to be united with all of us at home.

My hopes of going home with my baby were fading away by the next day. Zachary's oxygen was being decreased, and just when he should have been showing everyone that he could do it on his own, he started to crash. Alarms were ringing, doctors and nurses were flooding into the room. This was a nightmare that I wanted no part of. It couldn't be real or true.

The doctors stabilized Zachary, and worked on discovering the answer to why he was unhealthy. A heart murmur was detected, and x-rays were done. Dr. Mantynen indicated that there were serious problems with Zachary's little heart. He drew Mike and me a rough sketch of a disease I would come to know well. Hypoplastic Left Heart Syndrome sounded unbelievable. How could it be that our sweet boy has a congenital heart defect like this? We had done everything right. I had done nothing wrong during pregnancy, yet here we were, unsure if our infant son would ever know a life outside of this hospital.

Behind the grief we were feeling, Dr. Mantynen was making arrangements for Zachary's transfer to the world-renowned children's hospital in Toronto, Hospital for Sick Children. There a team of top cardiologists would assess his heart defect and provide us with a plan for action. As we prepared for this cruel twist, we contemplated the future of our family. We were uprooting Theo from a simple, happy life, to the unknown. Dr. Mantynen had explained that hypoplastic left heart was operable. A three-stage procedure was being used at top paediatric hospitals to repair and rebuild infants' hearts. The Norwood surgeries had been presented to us as the best possibility for Zach's survival.

The transport team from SickKids arrived to take Zachary with them. They worked to ensure that he was stable enough to travel, and took an instant photo of him for me. He looked so different from the photo that had been taken the day before. He looked sick. He had wires connected to him now. The nurses had given him a small blanket made by a volunteer. It was decided that Mike would travel with Zach in the ambulance to SickKids. I would go home to gather Theo, and a few belongings. Linda and Barry would join as we travelled to Toronto the next day to be with Mike and Zach. Our little family should have been home, sleeping, cooing, laughing, and changing newborn diapers. Instead we were separated. The Halloween candy discarded by the door. I couldn't bring myself to answer the bell as children came hoping to receive a treat.

Unfolding Truth

This was slowly starting to feel like a terrible reality. I was in pain from birth. I just wanted to be in bed resting with my newborn. Instead I was enduring a two-hour drive to the middle of a large city, to a hospital where my son had now been for the last 24 hours. I wanted to run and hide from this unfolding truth.

Mike had told us he'd be on the 2nd floor. The CCU. The Critical Care Unit. The waiting rooms there have boxes of tissues on the tables. Bleary-eyed parents sit, sometimes with other family members, sometimes on their own. Sometimes sleeping on the couches or in chairs with a lone rough sheet wrapping them against the chill of the hospital. Often weeping quietly. Sometimes weeping openly. I walked past, and saw Mike waiting.

It's mostly a blur. I was exhausted, and still in pain. Mike took me into the room where Zach was. He was in a room with three other beds. I can't even tell you who else was in the room. I walked straight to his crib. His little face was puffy. There seemed to be a million wires connected to him. IV pumps were on either side of his crib as well as a monitor following every heartbeat and every breath he took. There was another number on the screen that I wasn't familiar with. Over the next few days I would learn how important this number was, and this number would become a large part of my waking consciousness. I was so scared. This little being who was protected from everything while inside me was now lying in a crib covered in wires. I wanted to hold him, and protect him; take him back into my womb. I wanted to run with him to the life he deserved, not this life. Not the loneliness of a crib filled with medical interventions. I was told I could hold him. That scared me more. I didn't want to dislodge a life-saving intervention. How would I know how to handle this? I knew how to be a mom to a healthy baby. I didn't know how to be a mom to a medically fragile one. The nurses brought in a rocking chair and told me to sit down. They carefully lifted Zach out of the crib and laid him in my arms. The warm blanket that enveloped us contrasted with the tubes and wires that sustained his life. I had to hold a blue plastic tube close to his face. This tube now provided him with the very air of life. With Zach's heart as malformed and weak as it was, he couldn't handle normal room air. One hundred percent oxygen made his heart work too hard. This tube blew a special 'hypoxic-mix' of oxygen that allowed Zach's tiny heart to beat at a rate that kept him alive, and not in critical stress. For most, breathing in room air provides the lungs with the oxygen needed to feed the blood vessels. For a child born with HLHS like Zach, room air provides too much oxygen for the malformed heart to manage in its attempt to provide the necessary circulation. When not in my arms, Zach lay in his crib, all of his life-sustaining IVs, tubes and wires displayed around him, a plastic hood over his head surrounding him with his special oxygen mix.

In order to keep Zach's heart beating to the best of its ability in its malformed state, he needed to have saturations of 70-75. This number was critical, and I watched it like a hawk from this day and onward for the next nine and a half weeks.

It was time to meet with the cardiologists. After what we had been told in Cambridge, we were hopeful that the trio of surgeries would be happening as soon as possible. We wanted this to happen so that the healing and recovery could start. We wanted to be homeward bound. This, we would learn, would be far from the truth. We were led to a conference room off of the waiting room, where we were shown two seats at a table filled with doctors. Mike remembers feeling the awe of greatness in the room. I remember feeling scared, tired and sore. We met doctors Glen VanArsdale, Gil Gross and Lori West, all amazing individuals in the world of paediatric cardiology. I was waiting to hear when the first surgery would happen. Instead we were told that Zach's malformations were too great to do the surgeries. Dr. VanArsdale had done many of these surgeries, and he knew first-hand that this was not the option that would provide Zach with life. Dr. Gross described the complexities that hindered the repair and rebuilding that they had hoped to do. Instead we were offered two options: transplant or palliative care.

Stop.

I was sure that my heart, that my life, had just stopped. We were being asked to make a decision that held our newborn's life in the balance between life and death. If all the wires were removed, if the IVs were disconnected, if I picked up my son unencumbered from all of these, he would die. These wires, the IVs, the machines, were the ties holding him to us. These were the ties that were keeping him alive. These ties, however, were not permanent. What kind of life would he have, held by these ties? How could I even imagine burdening my child with these ties? Everything was a jumble in my mind. The lines were skewing. We had been pushed to the edge of the precipice of life and death. I heard Mike say, *yes. Yes. Whatever you have to do of course. Whatever it takes. We will do this.* He looked at me, and grasped my hand tighter. *We have to.*

The Wait

Adecision was made. Our baby lay in a crib. Not a comfy crib at home with soft lighting, but a hospital crib, in the critical care ward. Instead of a mobile spinning slowly playing lullabies over him, he was attached to machines that monitored his heart, his breathing, his blood pressure. Half of his tiny body was covered with a clear plexiglass square dome. If he were to breathe in too much room air, it would make his heart work too hard. This little walnut sized infant heart was not able to function as it should. There were intravenous tubes strung from him to machines that beeped and swished as life-saving medications dripped into his body. Medications that were keeping him alive for now. Within the first 20 hours after Zachary was born, a duct within his heart remained open. This is normal. Once the physical bond of the umbilicus is cut, the duct is supposed to close sometime after birth, allowing for the newborn's heart to function on its own. With this duct open, it masked the severe complications of his heart. Once it closed naturally, Zach's heart was unable to work as it should. Now, while waiting for his only chance to live, that little duct was being kept open with the aid of medication. To help his malformed heart pump, there was a different medication. He was also on calcium and potassium to help with heart function. He had an IV line in his umbilicus, which could only be used short-term. He would need a more stable long-term access for the duration of his hospitalization. They would insert a PICC line within days, which would allow for medications via IV as well as blood draws. The PICC line would go into a vein into his arm and snake through to his chest. With each of the medications there were risks. Without the medications he would die. Without a donor heart, he would not survive. This baby was our second child. He had been born with hypo-plastic left heart syndrome, a heart with a malformed left side, and a right side too weak to be transformed by surgeries to become a working whole. Each new piece of information, a harsh blow. We were told that ten out of every one hundred babies die waiting for a heart.

Zach's scheduled PICC line procedure happened and went well. As planned, he spent some time in the critical care unit before going back to his bed on the cardiac ward. The initial x-ray indicated that the line was perfectly placed; however, hours afterwards, Zach was experiencing episodes of tachycardia. His little heart was beating upwards of 200 bpm. Concern was starting to build, and as the tachycardic episodes weren't subsiding another x-ray was ordered. By the next day, the x-ray showed that the end of the line was too close to his heart. It was stimulating the rate, and needed adjustments. Thankfully, the procedure to remove, shorten and re-insert the line went well. Zach was back in his crib by that evening, and able to take a bottle from his dad.

With Zach's immediate medical difficulties we were thrust out of social connections and isolated by the medical world we then found ourselves in. For nine and a half weeks we waited. We waited by his crib. We waited in waiting rooms while he was having a procedure. We waited for someone to tell us that there was a heart for Zachary. We waited like vultures; such an awful feeling. I was angry that I was put in a position to make a decision about my child's mortality like this. I was heartbroken as I watched him. My newborn baby. I needed help just to pick him up and hold him. I couldn't feed him the way I wanted to. If I wanted a private moment with him, I had to draw a curtain around us. He would tire easily if he was in my arms for too long. I had to watch his monitor while I held him to ensure that his vitals were within a safe range. The wait was not uneventful. There were stretches of the walk on this precipice that had us hanging from the edge, often from only one or two fingers. Zachary spent most of his time waiting on the cardiology ward; however, those hanging moments were spent in CCU. Throughout the wait, his heart function would deteriorate enough that he would need small procedures to extend his ability to wait for the life-saving organ donation.

Our life had been turned upside down in a matter of days. We had been a family of three awaiting the birth of a new child. We were happy and in love with our almost two-year-old Theo. He was a bright ray of love in our lives. We couldn't wait to bring a sibling for Theo into our family. Now we were thrust into a medical world that frightened us. We were uprooted from our home, and living in a city that was big and bustling.

As a family facing such horrendous possibilities for their young baby, we were directed to Ronald McDonald House. This house would become our home. Our family unit had not just grown by one after Zachary's birth, but by three more, as we were joined in shifts by my sister and her husband, and my niece. They stayed with us before and after Zachary's transplant, supporting us, caring for Theo and being there…. just being there for us. We were being supported by many family and friends. Cards of support were coming in, messages of love and prayers for Zachary. Through Mike's musician community, two fundraisers were held to help us with expenses. Newspaper articles were written to help with support and also to bring awareness to the need for people to register as organ donors.

He's Stable

O ur life took on a new and monotonous existence. Any change to these days often meant that there was a change in Zach's health, which was never a positive thing. The only positive we were hoping for was the call that there was a heart.

Upon waking, I would spend time with Theo, and prepare to go to the hospital. My sister and her husband would plan a day of easy activities at RMH and in the neighbourhood to occupy Theo. I would walk to the hospital and spend the day at Zachary's bedside. I would pump breast milk to be frozen for him.

We had made a decision to accept a mismatched heart for Zachary if one became available. The Hospital for Sick Kids was on the cutting edge of infant cardiac transplants. Studies had been done from 1996-2000, and successful ABO mismatched transplants were increasing the survival rates of babies born with congenital heart defects. An ABO mismatch meant that a heart that was not the same blood type as the recipient could be accepted, as newborns have not yet begun to produce the antibodies that would reject a mismatched heart. Making the decision to accept such a heart would increase Zachary's chances to live. This, however, meant that he couldn't have my breast milk, as no studies had been done to ensure that a mother's antibodies wouldn't interfere with the success of a mismatched transplant. While this seemed an easy decision, as a breastfeeding mother this was so contradictory to my being. All the things that I loved and prepared for as I had anticipated the early weeks and months with my new baby were being stripped away. Zach had to be bottle-fed, and I did that whenever I could. The process for this was painstaking but worth it, to hold him and comfort him. I was sometimes able to bathe him, which was such a different experience to what I had looked forward to. All the wires and IV lines took precedence, for his health and safety. When he slept, I sat and took notes about his condition, his medications, and any new information of the day. I would sit and wait for doctors' rounds to hear if there were any new updates.

Theo would stay at RMH each day with my sister and her husband. Linda and Barry were unwavering in their support for our family. Each morning I would awaken hoping that today would be different. Each day, so much the same as the last. A routine developed. I would spend some time with Theo, waking up, readying myself for the hospital, breakfast together in the Ronald McDonald communal kitchen and dining room. Theo would be with me, helping, playing. Then I would leave. Walking to SickKids on my own. This was supposed to be a time when my little family was cocooned together, finding our path and falling in love together. Instead, my husband had to return home so that he could continue working, while I sat hour upon hour beside Zachary, waiting, never knowing if we'd ever all be together as we'd dreamed. Oftentimes, Linda and Barry would bring Theo to the hospital to visit with me and Zach. He stole the hearts of all he met. He was a complete charmer at the age of two. He seemed to take it all in stride. If asked "How is Zach?" Theo would reply, "He's stable." How innocent and crushing that one so young knew these words about his baby brother.

Days and weeks went by. It seemed an eternity. I found myself watching the news, and getting excited if there was a report on a deadly crash. Might there have been a child in that crash? God forgive me, I was waiting for another mother's child to die in order for mine to survive. It was the most mind-twisting, morality-shaking experience.

Each day was one day too many to wait. Each day, I felt I was being unfair to this sweet infant son, lying in a mass of wires and tubes, each second of his life hanging on the unknown. People would ask, "When will he get his heart?" A question so innocently asked. The question I could not answer. Would Zach be one of those who died waiting? We felt that we knew this place as though we had ourselves built it. We had walked almost every floor, save one; we had never walked out of the glass elevator onto the 8th floor, oncology. We knew that this floor was the space where children with cancer were treated. We had a mild understanding that here, the threat of germs was similar to that of a transplant patient.

After so many weeks of being away from our home in Cambridge, I decided that Theo and I would go home for a night. Mike was happy to have us home, but it was so difficult. I felt as though a large part of me was missing. I knew that Zachary was in good hands in the hospital. The wrenching feeling of being away from him was too much to handle. A few hours before our plan to head back to Toronto, the hospital called. The mixed feeling of excitement and dread filled me. Would this be the call that would save his life? After some routine blood work, it had been determined that Zachary would require a blood transfusion. While typically a safe and routine procedure, I felt ill that I wouldn't be there with him. I needed to get back to Toronto as soon as possible.

* * *

IVs needed to be moved frequently. This was done so that the sites didn't get too sore. Sometimes Zach's veins had collapsed. Each day it seemed there was something different. Yet each day seemed to mirror the last.

Zach often needed an NG tube to assist him with his feeds. Feeding is a tiring activity for babies, let alone a baby with a heart defect like Zach's. Having a nasogastric tube meant that he could get the needed nourishment without working too hard and causing cardiac distress. The thought that a necessity of life could be detrimental was dizzying. While Zach was getting the nutrients he needed, he would also often show signs of daily excessive weight gain. This edema was symptomatic of his heart deficiency, and was treated with lasix, to help his body rid itself of the excess fluid. It was all such a fine balance to keep this little life afloat.

The room that became home to Zach for the remainder of the year he was born was a room for four. It had its own nurses station, and there was always at least one nurse in the room at all times. My focus when I was there was Zachary. I did as much with him as I possibly could. When I wasn't caring for him or cuddling him, I was writing. It did become apparent at some point that there were three other children there too. Three children, three other sets of parents. One particular set-up across the room looked like a mirror image of Zach. Another little boy. A hood over his head to provide life-giving hypoxic mix. Was this little one waiting for a heart too? Eventually we spoke. Two moms, waiting and praying for what seemed an impossibility. This mom, though, had been through this before. While her little boy had the same heart disease as Zach, they knew ahead of time that he would need medical intervention, a transplant, to survive. Her firstborn, a girl, had been born with HLHS three years ago. Initial reparative surgeries had not gone well, and a heart transplant was necessary for her survival. Now, this little girl's brother was awaiting a transplant as well. What were the odds? The protective web I had spun around myself was pulled and ripped open and the world around me rushed in. We were not the only ones. Sick children everywhere. Children waiting for life-saving organs. A little boy like Zach who needed a heart too.

He was sicker than Zach. He was younger than Zach. The inner conflict that this created was unlike any feeling I had ever experienced. The complete contradiction filled my emotions. The caring I felt for this mother and family, against the desire to somehow ensure that Zachary's needs would be met first. The mother bear wanted to take over. Caring and compassion left me grieving the unknown possibilities for both of us. It was the most wrenching and agonizing feeling.

Eleven days later, I was told that a heart had been offered to this little boy. He needed it more than Zach did at this point. In a moment, one life can be quantified over another. My brain understood. My heart was breaking. Zach would make it. A heart for him would come. It would. I had to believe this. The wait went on. Zach was now first on the list.

* * *

Over thirty-nine days waiting. Each day running into the next. With the daily routine, each moment would hinge on Zach's wellness. The numbers and the signs. Every millilitre of fluid he took in was weighed against what he put out. HIs feeds, his medication, the IV fluid were all balanced to ensure he wasn't taking in too much fluid and working his little heart harder than it could bear. His vital signs were critical to making the decision between a bottle feed or a tube feed. Whether or not it was a good time to bathe him. Did he need more of one medication or treatment to help with his breathing, his heart rate, his oxygen levels? Was he feverish? Was he in pain? Why was he agitated?

One of Zach's heart defects was a hole between the left and right chambers of his heart. While waiting for a tiny heart to save his life, this hole was actually aiding in his survival. It could start to close on its own and, if this happened, a procedure would have to be done to open it. Slowly, each day there were minute signs that this was happening. Increased respirations. Increased oxygen in his blood, less need for the hypoxic mix were alluding to an inevitable. Over a few days, Zach was requiring medications for pain.

Intubation. A preventative measure, they said. They noticed that he was not bothered by the intrusive touch of having his vital signs taken. Then his oxygen saturation dropped to a very low 28. I was told that he never stopped breathing, his heart never stopped beating. He still had a blood pressure. X-rays echocardiogram and blood work being done. Checking for any possible infection, any answer, for this sudden and drastic turn. Zach was moved to the PICU within the hour. They were struggling despite all efforts to bring his oxygen levels up. Finally the echo showed that the ASD was indeed closing. Zach would need to have the procedure done to open it up, a balloon type device would be inserted into his heart in the Cardiac Catheter Lab to gently open up his ASD. While waiting another day for this to be done, another arterial IV line had to be put in to keep a closer look at his blood gases. Throughout all of this, morphine was keeping Zach sedated. As it turned out, the procedure would need to be moved up due to staffing complications. Once again we were agreeing to a procedure with multiple risks, but an outcome that would keep our little Zachary alive.

We were anxious for him. This was a 2-hour procedure. They started at 7PM. He made it through. He was recovering in the critical care unit. He was still intubated and sedated. He was so still.

By the next day, he was extubated, and seemed to be doing well. Nurses and respiratory therapists were hawks watching his vitals, and making tiny adjustments to ensure all of his systems were functioning well. Within a couple of days, he was able to be transferred back to the cardiac floor. With the ASD being expanded, he was able to breathe room air for longer blocks of time.

As I watched, comforted, and soothed Zach, they started him on continuous, slow feeding. He had now been without feeds for a few days, besides IV fluids. I started to notice that his legs were puffy, especially his left one, and seemingly painful for him. With increased swelling noted, he likely had a venous clot, a risk from the balloon procedure. He would need heparin injections to hopefully relieve it. The heparin would have to be administered by an injection every twelve hours. Thankfully, a small catheter was put into place so that the injections wouldn't be felt with each dose.

When I think of Christmas, I think of being at home with my family. This one was not like that. We were still at Sick Kids, still living in a room at RMH. Still separated from our home. We could at least be together. Somewhat. We did our best to provide a magical Christmas for Theo. Many volunteers provided activities, dinner, and gifts to residents at Ronald McDonald House. Zach had a visit from Santa at his cribside. We missed the visit, but a polaroid photo was left for us to see, as well as some gifts for Zach and Theo.

We were watching the calendar telling us that a year was coming to an end. Would Zach get his new heart before a new year began? The toll of waiting and watching my sweet boy live his life amidst the interventions of medicine was becoming unbearable. There was no relief.

As the days went on, Zach started to enjoy the sponge baths and immersion baths. Difficult as they were, we were in a rhythm. He loved having his hair washed, and loved the cuddles afterwards. We had crossed from December 2000 into January 2001 with little fanfare or change. We were still waiting.

During this time, we still had the help of Linda and Barry. Their daughter, my niece Mary, also became a pillar of support for us. When Linda and Barry couldn't be with us and had to make a trip back to their home in Nova Scotia, Mary would arrive within a day or so and stay to help us with Theo.

A Life to Give, a Life to Receive - 2001

Sixty-seven days. January 5th was sixty-seven days since Zachary had been born. On this day, a day that seemed like any other of these days that streamed past, a day in this unbelievable hell of days, the call finally came. I did not take the call. I was in the kitchen making coffee and breakfast with Theo and Mary. She had just arrived to help the night before. Mike came down from our room and told us that the transplant cardiologist had just called to tell us that a heart was available for Zach. I wanted to run. I felt like I needed to get to the hospital as soon as I could. I couldn't concentrate on anything else. My husband told me there was no rush. There would be plenty of time, as the heart was not yet at the hospital.

We were now waiting for the delivery of a heart. A walnut sized organ, packed in ice, to arrive from who knows where. Somewhere a family was grieving. They were grieving the loss of their child. And in that grief, they had chosen to give life. In a moment of death, they had chosen to give life to our son.

The heart was a perfect match; size and type. That meant that he could have my breast milk! Hours later, we waited. We had bathed him, and helped wheel him down to the operating room. It seemed an eternity as the surgeons, scrub nurses and anesthesiologists came out to meet us and tell us what they planned to do.

* * *

A complete blur. My mind tries to pull at the wisps of memories. My mind is protective of me. It has buried trauma. A slight tug brings the reels of my memories to light. It was at night, and we were led to a small family room off of the surgical waiting room, where we were told we could rest while we waited. They operated through the night. Moments of exhausted sleep interrupted by insane worry dotted the night. Lying in the dark. My body had grown and nurtured two beings. Two hearts made by me and Mike were beating outside our bodies. Now we lay here, with neither of these beautiful flesh bodies close to us. Theo was at RMH with Mary. At 10PM Zach was lying on an operating table having his heart replaced. Somewhere, another family mourned their child.

* * *

Each vessel, each artery, the aorta, was sewn in with precision and accuracy. This took hours of meticulous skill to complete. Once his new heart was beating in his body, they would do an echocardiogram to make sure that it was working well. We were exhausted and exuberant. The days of waiting had come to an end and we were on the other side. Now the recovery could begin. Then the echo results were in. We were told that although this new heart was seemingly working well, there did seem to be a minor issue. We were told that the heart had a left bundle branch block. This sounded devastating. Block. Block. Not a word you want to hear following a surgery that was supposed to be life-saving. We were reassured by the cardiologists that they were not concerned. This, in their expertise, was a minor issue.

They were still in the operating room, and preparing to move to recovery in critical care when his blood pressure was indicating issues with the heart. As his pressure dropped, we were told that the new heart was reacting to the trauma of being removed and on ice. Zach would have to be put back on the ECMO or Heart Lung Machine to give his heart a chance to reheat. While this complication is not unexpected, it is not what they hope for, but not outside the norm.

By 5:30 the next morning, we were told that Zach was in the critical care unit, and would be for some time. While the new heart had taken a while to warm and beat on its own, it was now working better and better with time.

I had a vague memory of a nurse coming in through the night and saying, "It's a gorgeous little heart."

Critical

H e was so still. His chest was open and covered by a sheet of gauze. He was attached to even more machines, tubes and wires then he had been when he was waiting. He was stable, but still so critical. It was as though he were a part of the machines that were now helping him to live. I couldn't hold him. We had waited for this day and now it seemed a horrific mistake. Our boy lying like this, medically stilled for survival. It was a system shock. The medical staff were pleased and positive. I had to believe that he would recover. A new chapter had been opened.

"I can't move, but I can hear you. I may be awake. I can feel you."

These words were taped to the head of Zach's bed in critical care, and reminded me each moment why we were here. His medications and vitals were monitored closely. Whenever possible or necessary, changes were made to ensure his health and recovery. He was being given my breast milk through his NG tube. High-calorie powder was being added to help him thrive. They would decrease the muscle relaxants in hopes that he could be more awake. This often led to him being very alert. While this was good news, it was dangerous due to his open chest, and the machines he was attached to.

We learned that Zachary's new heart had been outside of a body for 4 hours and 36 minutes until it was beating inside his body. In order to be moved from the critical care ward, Zach would have to be extubated, have his chest closed, and be off all of the medications except the anti-rejection or immunosuppression ones.

Rocky Recovery

Zach's recovery was nothing short of rocky. We were still on the precipice. The transplant had gone well, but we were still dangling on the edge. By four days post transplant, his chest was still open, but would hopefully be closed by the next day. There were many adjustments to his immunosuppressive meds, as it is critical that the heart is not rejected.

It was noticed that there was likely a leak from Zach's lymphatic system. Following complicated surgeries, the body needs assistance with draining. The drainage vessels were showing some fatty substance. This was probably a nick that happened during the transplant surgery. The drainage of chyle into his chest cavity, a rare condition known as chylothorax. As well, Zach's kidneys weren't functioning as well as they should so he was on a modified dialysis. He was retaining a lot of fluid, so this procedure would help to absorb waste fluids that weren't being cleared out by his kidneys, and also take out any extra fluid to alleviate his edema. During this procedure, some of the fluid leaked into Zach's sternum. This needed to be cleaned out by surgeons. Once this was done they hoped to close his chest cavity.

I had come that day, as any day, to visit with Zach. Now I was sitting in the waiting room, as I couldn't see him while they worked on him. I sat and prayed that all would go well. Within a few hours I was told I could go in. Finally, his chest cavity was closed! This was a good step towards recovery. As he was weaned off the muscle relaxants, he became more and more alert. His big wide eyes peered into mine, and he squeezed my finger when I put it in the grasp of his tiny fingers. He was still intubated. We were so hoping to soon move towards this critical step in his recovery. Zach's little body was still puffy from the trauma of the surgery and transplant. The nick in his lymphatic system would take time to heal. Due to the swelling, his incision was not closing as it should, so would possibly need to be restitched at some point. To add to these complications, chylothorax meant that he could no longer take the breast milk that had been frozen and saved for him. The formula that they put him on was not being tolerated by his little tummy. They would tell me that these things were not uncommon. How wonderful that the difficulties were normal. Another brain hurdle.

After a week, we were hopeful that Zach could be extubated, and that one of his chest tubes could be removed. This meant that it would be possible for him to be held. What a milestone. Sometimes a step forward results in a step back. The removal of catheters and tubes meant sedation, and this meant an increase in his ventilator. While we were anxious for him to be without the breathing tube, x-rays showed that his lungs were still a bit wet, so to be cautious they would hold off.

Ten days following his transplant, Zach was extubated. As a precaution, he was put back under the respiratory hood. This felt like a step backward. My mind couldn't let go of the idea that this heart wasn't working as it should. Why would he still need this chamber? Yes, it had kept him alive the months leading up to transplant, but I wanted desperately for Zach to be past this. I wanted him, needed him, to be well. I hoped that this was merely a precaution. That this new little heart would be fine. The next step would be nasal prongs as he'd be weaned off oxygen supplement completely. By the following day, I was able to hold him. He was very content to be held, but his surgical wound was leaking a fair bit. He was coughing a lot, a good sign as it helps to clear out the lungs. His kidney function at this time was not very good and doctors were quite concerned. One of the usual immunosuppressants is very toxic for the kidneys. Unfortunately this medication was a standard in the heart transplant protocol and could not be changed. My mind traced back to the day we were given the option of transplant. All of the information that had been thrown at us. "Transplant is not a cure. It comes with its own difficulties. Setbacks due to being immunocompromised, side-effects of the meds can lead to other serious medical issues." Here was one of those issues. His kidneys had taken a hit from the surgeries and heart function, complicated ever more with the medication. Not even two weeks after his life-saving transplant, Zacharay was in dire condition. While heart function was good, to make matters worse, he had a high white blood count which could mean infection or rejection.

Now it was a balancing act to keep Zachary hydrated, while ensuring that his fluid levels didn't overload his suffering kidneys. He needed antibiotics for what seemed to be an infection. X-rays and ultrasounds still showed fluid in his lungs, and his chest cavity was still requiring drainage, so another chest tube was inserted. It was feeling that we were taking steps backwards now. Zach's situation was worsening. So many things were changing so quickly. He was also put on a very high caloric venous infusion for his feeds. Total Parenteral Nutrition (TPN) would put the nutrients Zach needed directly into his body, bypassing his gastrointestinal system. He would be able to have small feeds of the formula for now through the NG tube.

We were told that kidney specialists, nephrologists, would be consulted to review his current issues. While there were differing conclusions at first regarding his kidney function, it was determined that they were, at the very least, the right size and in the proper place.

The insertion of the new chest tube was followed by a gush of extra fluid draining from the chest cavity. There was some blood loss at first, then the flow seemed to settle. Having this fluid drain helped with Zach's oxygen levels, and he wasn't struggling to breathe as much. By the next day there was some improvement with his urine output, but not much. Important indicators were showing that there was still concern. He needed a blood transfusion following the blood loss after the chest tube drainage the day before. As nurses worked tirelessly to ensure all of his needs were balanced, Zach's oxygen saturations suddenly dropped. They quickly turned up his oxygen intake, and did some blood work. The results showed that his blood acid levels were high and in need of some bicarbonate. We were learning just how intricate our body systems are, and about their need to work together. As his kidneys continued to be in crisis, the effects were being shown in his blood, his lungs, and his heart. Chest cavity fluid was an increasing issue, and one of the chest tubes would need to be replaced. Zach was placed on CPAP to ease his breathing. He needed frequent suctioning to rid him of thick mucus that was impeding his lungs. The thought was that the nick to his lymphatic system was the cause of the persistent fluid and chyle in his lungs. Zach was no longer able to feed even by NG tube. His only nutrition was coming from TPN.

The following 16 days were spent in the CCU. Zach had a string of infections that made him crampy and feverish. Each day was met with a new development in his care. All bodily functions were being weighed, measured, and tested. Organ functions were monitored frequently through ultrasounds and x-rays. Blood and urine were tested to ensure that the workings of this tiny body were functioning well enough for him to survive. IV lines were moved and changed on what seemed a daily basis. Sometimes, these lines were sources of infection. Infections were treated with antibiotics. And antifungal medications were added to deter growths. Zach's need for oxygen would fluctuate daily, depending on so many variables. He would either be on CPAP or nasal prongs. My knowledge of medical terms was quickly growing and I felt I could pass any nursing test.

Part of life with a donated organ involves many tests and procedures to ensure that the organ is not being rejected by the body. At the time, the protocol required Zachary to undergo biopsies quite frequently. While still in CCU during his recovery, Zach had his first biopsy on January 19th 2001. He would have to be sedated and intubated for this procedure. This was the first of so many biopsies done. By all counts it went well. There were a few anomalies, for which they had an answer.

Within a day of his biopsy, Zach was uncomfortable, discontent, and showing signs of an infection. He was still on many antibiotics. It was incredible how each bacteria required its own medication to rid it from the body. This one was an opportunistic one. It was likely caused by his recent intubation. It was also thought that his PICC line was a source of infection, and would need to be replaced.

Zach had also been on morphine since his transplant, and they were starting to wean him from it after nineteen days. It was hoped that he could be off of it in a few days. Another infection was identified in his lungs, but he was already on an antibiotic that would take care of it. Each day I would hold him if I could. He was now able to take feeds through his NG tube again. It was a bit of a trick to find the right flow rate so as not to fill his little belly too quickly. With all of these complications, Zach was showing little signs of his sweet personality. His smile and bright eyes warmed my heart and my being.

His little limbs, however, were indicating that he needed to move more. After being sedated, and on muscle relaxants in those critical first days, his legs were in contracture. We would do exercises each day to help stretch his legs and arms. He would need chest physiotherapy as well, as he continued to recover. Having the chest cut open meant that all of those muscles would need help to strengthen and repair.

It felt as though Zach would be in the CCU forever. The recovery had been far from easy. We longed to be past this incredibly difficult phase. As my strength wavered, my heart held on, staying by his side, helping with any and all therapies that I could participate in. Forever grateful for the expertise of the doctors and nursing staff.

6th Floor

After almost three weeks in the critical care unit we were given the news that a transfer would happen. Finally, Zach might be well enough to take the next step in his recovery. We had now been at Sick Kids with him for 87 days. The thought of going home seemed almost like a dream. We were hopeful, encouraged, and exhausted.

The prospect of taking that next step however was dashed when Zach was diagnosed with yet another infection. This time it was a gastrointestinal bug that caused severe diarrhea. Torovirus was apparently sweeping through the hospital. Zach's move to the transplant recovery ward on the sixth floor would be postponed. He was moved to a different room in CCU with two other children also with Torovirus. We were now wearing full gowns and masks to visit with Zach to ensure we didn't contract the virus or take it out of the room.

The constant monitoring and tests continued, with good reason. An echocardiogram to take a look at Zach's heart function showed that there was an extra beat. Zach's new little heart was now showing slight signs of rejection. We were told that this was common. Perspective is everything. With a new cardiac transplant parent, you don't want to think about let alone hear that there could be organ rejection. Tweaks in his immunosuppressive meds were made to fight the rejection. His chest tubes were still draining, but more slowly now. An x-ray showed that the fluid was diminishing, but now there were pockets of air; pneumothorax; to add to the complications. It was almost a full week before Zach was cleared of the gastro virus and able to move out of the CCU.

We settled into this new room, but it was unsettling at the same time. A big part of recovery was the push to the next level. It was overwhelming. To the doctors and nurses who did it every day, it was commonplace. Zach still had many medical issues to overcome. He still had one chest tube in. He still had an extra heartbeat, and he still had pneumothorax. Zach was also still receiving daily injections for the venous clot that had been caused by the balloon dilation before his transplant. He was still receiving nutrition through his PICC line, and gastro feeds were slowly being reintroduced. There was no longer a nurse in the room with us. This was a room for Zach and Zach alone. One crib, and a bench seat that I could sleep on. This first night he was very uncomfortable and the source seemed to be the chest tube. Poor baby was also still very stiff. His knees, shoulders and neck were all painfully inflexible. His physiotherapist helped to ensure that he was getting positioned for optimal comfort.

The pain Zach was experiencing from the chest tube increased when the tube dislodged. It was repositioned by a vascular surgeon. Within a few hours though, Zach was in obvious excruciating pain. Thankfully I was able to track down his vascular surgeon, who did a quick x-ray which showed that the tube was placed too far inside the chest wall. Such pain for Zachary. While Zach was still in his crib, the surgeon repositioned the tube. Zach showed immediate relief. He was still upset, however, and started to show signs of a fever. He was given pain relievers and Tylenol for some much needed consolation. These days and nights were like a new crash course in medical parenting. A nurse was available when we needed, but not beside us to constantly observe and tweak as we had become accustomed.

After a bit more drainage and another repositioning, the last chest tube was finally removed a week later. It was such a combat of feelings as each day Zach had to fight to get well again. I was feeling the effects of one hundred days in a hospital with an infant. It seemed that at his very young age of three months, Zach too was tired of it. One morning when he was having blood drawn, his little hand reached over and pulled out the blood work needle. Everyone was shocked!

The walls and floors of the hospital were all too familiar to us. I could barely remember what it was like to live in our small family home back in Cambridge. People would tell me that I was the epitome of calm. Each day since Zachary's birth I had kept it together, knowing that I had to be the strength to get him through this. Feeling that any inability on my part to cope would be his undoing. This little soul needed his mother for strength and resilience. It was around this time that I stumbled upon a quote that would sum up the way I would move through the rest of my life as a parent.

Courage is not the absence of fear, but rather the judgement that something else is more important than fear.
~ Ambrose Redmoon

A Time for Home

Sometime in March, we were given a weekend pass to go home. After Zach's transplant on January 5, we had moved into a 'hospital apartment' to wait out Zach's recovery. It was a small one-bedroom apartment in a building directly across the street from SickKids. The apartment was made available to out of town families who would need to stay in the city for an extended length of time. Following almost 70 days at Ronald McDonald House, we were glad to be able to have a space that was closer to the hospital, where we could one day bring Zach as we prepared for him to be taken home. Mike had been mostly living in our Cambridge home, continuing with his work, and travelling to be with us each weekend.

Theo was thrilled to have his little brother with him. He snuggled and cuddled him. How beautiful it was to see them together after so many months of having the hospital bed, and so many tubes, holding them apart.

Mary had moved into the apartment with us, and spent the days with Theo while I continued to spend my days with Zach. Now that the wait was over, things were feeling a bit less stressful. It was wonderful to have Mary with us, and she and Theo created quite a bond.

Following a lengthy recovery, and in-hospital training for me to be able to manage Zach's medical needs in a home environment, he was discharged to the apartment to live with us. It was scary. Zachary was required to take many immunosuppressant drugs so that his body wouldn't reject the life- saving organ he had received. He also had to take medications to counteract some of the side effects he might have from the immunosuppressants. In total, there were nine medications, a few of them four times a day. He needed to keep the nasogastric tube in to ensure that he received enough nutrients to grow. The medications could be put through the NG tube, but the goal would be that the meds would be tolerated orally, so that when the NG tube was no longer needed, he'd be somewhat used to them. When a child has a critical heart condition, feeding is a tiring endeavour. An NG tube is a necessity for growth and life, but an infant will quickly develop oral aversions, if they don't have anything in their mouths. It was imperative that Zach get some kind of oral stimulus for survival. He had had an NG tube for a number of months, and now I had to run the pump, as well as try to get him to feed by mouth. Each day we would walk to the hospital for Transplant Clinic. I carried Zach in the sling that had carried Theo for so many months. Any parent knows that taking an infant anywhere requires you to carry a diaper bag along. An excursion away from home means bringing anything that might possibly be needed with you. Zach's diaper bag also included many medications as well as his feeding pump. I carried all of this along with us each day. These visits often included tests like echocardiograms, or ECGs as well as check-ups from the nurses and nurse practitioners with the transplant program. It was at one of these visits that I cried to an echo tech. The strain of having a medically fragile child, trudging through the cold and slush of Toronto's winter with all of the medical paraphernalia was taking its toll on me. How would I be able to take care of this baby with all of the extra medical needs and equipment as well as continue with the life we had had, a toddler, two dogs? It all seemed impossible.

Mary had been with us for a number of weeks, and it was time for Linda and Barry to give her some respite. They arrived as Mary left, and took over Theo's daily care. One day, Barry said he wanted to take

Theo on a bit of a tour. He had decided to take him to the Hockey Hall of Fame. Theo was always happy to go anywhere with Uncle Boo, so following a bran muffin for breakfast, Barry and Theo went off on their excursion. The weather was cold, so Theo had worn multiple layers that included an outer rain suit. It zipped from chin to heel. When they returned, Barry regaled us with stories of their travels. Theo, we realized, had quietly gone to stand behind the drapes at the patio door of the apartment. I recalled that he looked a little ashen when they had come in, but was distracted by the laughs and the stories. As Theo came out from behind the drapes, we soon understood why he had taken some time alone. As the smell started to permeate the room, I began to unzip one layer of Theo's suit, and quickly decided that this needed to be done in the bathroom. Soon Theo was rinsed and soaking in a bubble bath. The chant that Uncle Barry was now reciting would become a long-time joke; "Thank you for not pooping at the Hockey Hall of Fame."

* * *

When we were told we could go home for a weekend, it was a frightening yet exciting concept. Travelling with a baby at the best of times is a daunting task for many parents. We packed up the van and drove the two hours to Cambridge. The weekend was tiring, and surreal. It was still winter and I felt closed in and alone. The house seemed foreign. Ensuring that Zach had all of his medical necessities consumed me. I felt I had to do all of the things I had done before, as well as the duties bestowed upon me as the parent of this fragile child. It was overwhelming to say the least. In many ways I couldn't wait to get back to Toronto and the safety of the hospital environment.

Weekends are short when you have young kids. They're even shorter when there's travelling involved. Add in all of the equipment that Zachary required, and we were left with a short time before we were required to return. The following day, I took Zach to Transplant Clinic, and we were told that he was doing so well that we would be discharged home. What? You're sending us home? I was in disbelief. It was a tumultuous undertaking. Being close to the hospital was a real safety net. The thought of being home was daunting. Was I capable of doing all of this?

Zachary still required weekly clinic appointments, tests and biopsies. Having a transplanted organ comes with a myriad of difficulties. As we were told from the beginning, transplant is not a cure. By agreeing to a transplant, we understood that we were in essence trading one disease for another. Being immunosuppressed meant that Zachary would be more susceptible to illness. A regular cold would send him to the hospital with pneumonia. A childhood disease, that most thought to be a rite of passage, could be fatal. We had to be very vigilant about any exposure to illness, especially chicken pox. Zach could not receive many of the scheduled vaccines that other children would receive, leaving him open to rather than safe from diseases like measles, mumps and rubella. Zachary would also be more susceptible to many cancers. It was not outside the realm of thinking for me to worry and wonder, what kind of life had we provided for our child. As a parent, you expect to think about your child growing, thriving, learning, and enjoying life. You should be thinking about their character, their future, and their happiness. Instead we were left in a constant state of worry. Would the next outing result in an unexpected sickness due to exposure? Was he meeting his developmental milestones?

Setback

Each time Zach was scheduled for a routine biopsy, he had to go without eating or drinking for twelve hours before the procedure. For an infant, there is no understanding of why they are being refused food and drink. Quite often, biopsies would be delayed or postponed due to the needs of other patients. Completely understandable, but very difficult to manage for a hungry baby. Each time, the protocol included pre-op visits from cardiac surgeons and anesthesiologists to ensure that Zach was physically able to have the procedure done, and that I was aware of the risks involved. Imagine putting your child into the hands of a skilled surgical team multiple times before they reached the milestone of their first birthday. Imagine doing that following the explanation of how many things could go wrong after you left the room.

Each time, I was permitted to walk into the cath-lab with Zach and lay him on the cold metal table. Over time, he became very familiar with the routine. It was often commented that he was so good, and calm. I would hold his hand, kiss his forehead, and silently pray. The nurses would make small talk, and gently direct me where to stand, and when to leave. As I moved to leave, they would be covering his little mouth with a mask. The anesthetic would start to work, his breathing would steady. He surely cried when he was a baby. It was absolutely heart-breaking to walk out of the lab, not knowing whether one of the risks would somehow smash its way into our lives. I would make my way to the food court. I made it a point to never eat in front of Zach while he was fasting for a procedure. In those early days, the surgical waiting room was for families waiting for news on any surgery or procedure. It was a mixing pot of people looking extremely worried and exhausted. Everyone here was awaiting news about a child's health status. I watched for a familiar face to walk towards me. I watched body language in hopes of a hint of the news about to be shared.

During one of the routine biopsies, Zachary went into heart-block. It had only been a couple of months since his transplant. We were told that Zachary had to be sedated and muscle relaxed, as he now had an external pacemaker ensuring that his heart was beating as it should. It was explained that during the biopsy, the little snips and tests had caused Zachary's heart to go into atrioventricular block. The bundle branch block that was discovered when the heart was transplanted was proving to be a serious problem. The electrical signals inside the heart were not firing as they should. In order to keep Zach's heart beating, the external pacer was in place. They were hopeful that his heart just needed to recover from the shock and would be fine in time. While Zachary was once again in Critical Care, I moved Theo and myself to Toronto. There wasn't any room at RMH, so we were given a room at the college dorms across from the hospital. These rooms were spartan at best, but we were grateful for somewhere to sleep. Nephew Sean came to stay and look after Theo while I made my daily trek to the critical care unit to sit with Zach. Seeing him muscle sedated again was a lot to bear. All I could do was hope and pray that the doctors were right.

After a few days, and some tests, however, the concern was growing. As Zach's heart didn't seem to be rebounding from this setback, it was decided that an internal pacemaker would be the best option. We knew that the heart transplant was not going to be a cure, that it was an exchange for a host of health issues. The worry that one of the disclosed risks would crash through had happened. Zach was taken once again into surgery, so that an internal pacemaker could be inserted.

Following Zach's setback and recovery, we were back home. Zach still required a tremendous amount of medical care along with the regular care and infant needs. Home care by way of physiotherapy, dietary, occupational therapy, and nursing all visited our home each week. Visits to Clinic in Toronto were at least every 2 weeks. The list of clinics to visit now included pacemaker, as the unit itself would need to be checked and data was downloaded so that they could view how frequently his heart needed to be electronically paced at a normal rhythm. As Zach grew and developed, things were never easy. We had conditioned ourselves to feel that what we encountered was part of the norm. Our lives would never be the same as the result of his birth. It was our life and our love. Survival was contingent on our ability to be resilient in the face of the medical fragility of our son.

Our lives settled into our own pattern of usual. This pattern became etched into days and months. We began to reconnect with friends, and despite all of the trauma, we were enjoying life with two little boys. The neighbourhood was a series of perpendicular streets lined with small wartime homes, perfect for new families. As we ventured out, there were friends to make, games to be played, and fun to be had. Visiting with Dagmar, Russell, Rob and Lena was always a treat. They had a large property, fields that they rented out for crops, an old farmhouse that they continued to renovate as they were able, space to enjoy many outdoor contraptions, and their own forest of trails. Many days were spent with the kids enjoying plasma cars in 'Big Red,' the barn out back, dirt bikes, and snowmobiles. The kids ran, played and laughed together. One summer we used some of their garden space and planted some vegetables. What fun it was to grow brussels sprouts, broccoli and sugar snap peas, when we didn't have that kind of space on our own property.

* * *

It was raining. One of those early summer rains, the air heavy with the humidity. Zach had been doing well. Our life was like a hitch between hospital stays. We would grasp onto these moments, try to hold on and build some stability. I picked him up, and called to Theo. "Let's go!" I smiled. Theo recognized the look in my eyes. We grabbed a few towels and dropped them unceremoniously by the back door. With Zach on my hip in the sling, and Theo's hand in mine, we rain out into the rain. We laughed as we ran up and down the street, ensuring to make the most of each splash, finding every pooling puddle the downpour was creating. A rain like this was an invitation to put everything else aside and live in that moment. Back inside, we would wrap ourselves in the towels. I helped the boys shed their wet clothes and wrap up again, cuddling on the couch, giggling and winded from our run, still enjoying the moment we had created.

Halloween

We were never ready for Halloween. It always seemed a last-minute rush to get the treats, and have them ready at the door. The first year that I recall Theo being ready for Halloween, he was dressed in a costume that I don't recall, and we were trying to encourage him that it was time to head out the door to visit the houses on our street. He, however, was more interested in staying by our front door, awaiting the trick-or-treaters who would arrive on our porch. He wanted to be the one who gave out the candy.

When Zach and Theo were four and two, I came across an article in the paper about Kans for Kids. This local grassroots organization was started by a young boy after one year asking his mom why some homes in his neighbourhood didn't give out candy at Halloween. His mom explained that not all families were able to afford the cost of treats, and perhaps even struggled to put food on their tables. This boy thought about the implications of this, and the next Halloween said he wanted to collect food for families who didn't have enough.

This project grew from year to year. By the time we had read about it, it was likely five years in. Many other families had joined in and become gatherers for the cause. The idea was to collect food for the food bank on Halloween night instead of collecting treats. We decided that we would join the task and set out to collect canned goods on Halloween night. I think we continued this tradition for at least five years. The first year, with Theo and young Zach, we pulled a wagon to collect the food our neighbours contributed. The wagon was overflowing! The next year, we borrowed a shopping cart from Sobeys! Each year, we would print a flyer and deliver it to the neighbourhood to let them know we'd be hoping to find some boxed or canned food when we rang their doorbell. Each year, our little community didn't disappoint. It became a little tradition, and one we remember fondly!

Thoughts of Another - 2002

E ventually as Zach grew, we became accustomed to our lives, with all of his medical needs. We felt that perhaps we could be brave enough to have another child. I'm sure there were many who thought we were out of our minds. Were we being selfish to have another? Were we putting an unborn child at risk before it had even been conceived? We had done some genetic testing and learned that HLHS could possibly be genetic. We knew that the possibility of having another child with the same heart defect was a slight risk. During one of Zach's routine clinic visits, I casually mentioned that we were considering having another child. Mirna, our clinic nurse, exclaimed enthusiastically that she thought it was a great idea, and that she could see us as a family of five.

I soon felt the familiar flutterings of life taking root in my womb, and we felt as though this was a natural move forward. We were in love with the idea of having another baby. In love, and petrified. The news seemed to hang in the air precariously as each day inched forward. Having a family with two boys was wonderful, and the idea that there may be a girl developing gave us a new feeling of what our family would be.

Zach was not quite two years old, and Theo was almost three. We decided to take a trip to Nova Scotia. I would fly down with the boys, and Mike would drive down after a week or so to meet us. It was wonderful visiting with my mom and sisters. Theo and Zach got to meet and enjoy their cousins, aunts, uncles and gramma. Gatherings with old high school friends melted away the years and miles between us. We laughed and sang as though no time had passed.

Mike had driven our van to Nova Scotia in a record 21 hours, stopping periodically for relief and to stretch. He had brought Sheila with him, so she ensured that he would stop with a quick whine and lick to the arm. He had also brought the camping gear, so we set off to Prince Edward Island for the night. In retrospect, I suppose we should have been more cognizant of what the weather forecast held for the island. I knew that it was always windy there, as you are never far from the ocean. We weren't prepared for torrential rainfall. We took the Confederation Bridge over to the island, which for a born and bred Maritimer like me was such an incredible feat, having only been able to get to the island by ferry up until 1993. We drove to the KOA on the West River, just outside of Charlottetown, and set up our tent. It was almost like a repeat of what had happened to Mike and I when we had travelled through New England just before we were married. Not long after supper, the usual gentle island breeze started to pick up. Our site was right on the edge of the river which opens up to the Charlottetown Harbour. It wasn't too far to walk to the dunes to explore at the waterfront. We made our way back to the site, and started to get ready for the night. The breeze had turned into wind, and it now held drops of rain as it whipped around. We tried so hard to stay for the night, believing that it would eventually die down. Soon enough, however, our bedding was soaking wet, there was a new river being forged through our tent, and we could barely hear each other through the pounding of the rain and the wind. We packed up the van and left the KOA in search of a motel. As Mike drove, I was on the phone calling any local motel I could find. In our quest to ride out the storm, however, we had been left in the dust of all the other campers who had bailed much sooner than we had. There were literally no rooms to be found for miles. At some point, a kind soul of a desk clerk suggested that we try the university. Luckily, it was close, so we pulled up to the University of PEI in search of dry beds for the night. For one hundred dollars we were able to get two spartan rooms for the night. Mike took Sheila with him, and I took Theo and Zach. We each had a room that housed one single bed and one desk and chair. It was warm and dry, and would at least afford us a bit of sleep for the night. The following day was bright and sunny, with little sign that there had been a storm the night before. We drove the short route back to the campsite after getting something to eat in Charlottetown. Our tent had remained standing throughout the night, but would definitely not have been a good source of shelter from the storm. We packed up, did a bit of sightseeing around the island, and made our way towards the Wood Island Ferry to return to Nova Scotia.

It truly was wonderful to be experiencing and sharing my home province as well as other Atlantic Canada sights with my young family. After a bit of a rest at Mom's place in Truro, we travelled from Truro to Bridgetown with the intent to visit with Linda and Barry for a couple of days. The expanse of their property in this Nova Scotia village provided a lovely sense of calm and connection to the outdoors. Gardens full of flowers and meandering paths down to a cherry tree close to the Annapolis River evoked the feeling that we had been afforded a stay in paradise (which, ironically, is the name of a little village just east of Bridgetown). Theo was as excited to meet so many of his older cousins, and was thrilled that cousin Mike wanted to take him fishing. They collected some worms from a few digs of a shovel in the garden, and carefully put them into a container for bait. It was a beautiful sight to see these two walk down the driveway with poles in hand, heading to the brook. Not too long afterwards, they returned with the poles, but no sign of any success in using them. With a smirk, Mike proceeded to tell us how he and Theo had made it to the brook, discussing along the way how the earthworms would be 'food' for the fish. They would put the worms on hooks and place their hooks in the water in hopes that the fish would be hungry and 'bite.' When they arrived at the brook, Mike set about putting worms on their hooks, and Theo proceeded to feed the fish by dumping the remaining worms into the brook. This of course cut the fishing trip significantly short, and they enjoyed the walk back to the house.

I was starting to experience an uncomfortable ache in my abdomen while we visited with Linda and Barry. The cramping, subsequent symptoms, and verification from a doctor at the local hospital confirmed that this baby would not be born. As we quietly mourned the loss of this life, we believed that something had occurred as the forming of cells split and grew in nature's plan. The cells' division and development were not strong enough to survive.

While I recovered physically and mentally from this miscarriage, we were preparing to drive back to Ontario. We weren't entirely sure if we were ready for this trip, but we certainly couldn't turn back at this point.

Our camping gear had survived the deluge of rain in PEI, so we decided to stop in New Brunswick, just outside of Woodstock, on our way home. We found a place called Jellystone Park, which sounded like a fun adventure for our family. There were waterslides as well as other amenities to enjoy. As campers, however, we were not prepared for the experience that this place had to offer. We were used to State, Provincial and National Parks that provided very natural surroundings. At this point we weren't deep woods campers, but we did enjoy the privacy that the government run parks delivered. What a different experience at a place like Jellystone! They ensured through the size of their sites that as many families as possible could be jammed in cheek by jowl. There was no choice in whether or not to be neighbourly, as we felt as though we were living in each other's space. As we set up our site, we soon became aware of the theme of this park. Within a half hour of arriving, there was an announcement over the loudspeaker informing everyone within at least a mile of any upcoming activities. We knew that this was a one-night-only stop, so settled in as best we could, and enjoyed some of the activities at the park. After supper and a fire, we settled in for the night a little later than the boys, hoping for a good sleep before heading out by noon the next day. We all slept soundly until seven the next morning, when we were loudly awakened by the loudspeaker announcing the dawn to all the campers. It was an experience straight out of summer camp. "Good morning Jellystone Campers! On the agenda today, …" Well we laughed and laughed! We have never gone back, but we have never forgotten the startling awakening at Jellystone.

We continued our drive into Quebec, and decided to stop at Old Quebec City. We wandered the streets and enjoyed the old-world charm of this city. Each step, we were loving the experience of being a young family, hopeful for the future, grateful for our boys, and grateful for life.

Reflecting on Bonding - 2003

A s life continued, the shock of what we had already encountered in the first five years of our marriage was slowly being pushed down as we created new and happy memories. Zach and Theo were enjoying brotherhood. Zachary was stronger each day. He was now almost two years old. He no longer needed the feeding tube. We still saw specialists to help with his physical development. Visits to SickKids would continue frequently. By January of 2003 I was pregnant again. This time, the tiny life inside me grew to full term. We decided that we would have a fetal echo done to prepare ourselves for the possibility of congenital heart disease. We were elated to learn that the baby girl I was carrying had a healthy heart!

We decided to take a trip to Terrace Bay that summer. Mike's father Fred and his stepmother Diane lived there. Mike hadn't grown up with his dad, but had forged a relationship in adulthood. It was a wonderful feeling to connect our children with their father's side of the family. The drive was extensive, especially with our young boys, and my pregnancy. We arrived late at night, visiting first at the hunting camp that Fred and Diane stayed at each summer. The beauty of Northern Ontario lay just steps outside the camp. Wabikoba Lake was pristine most days, with small waves lapping the edge of the shore being the only sound. We indulged in this escape from the city for a few days, Zach and Theo enjoying the best that nature provided. Boat rides with Grandpa included a bit of fishing. After a few days, we followed Fred and Diane into Terrace Bay to stay at their home over the July 1st holiday before heading back to Southern Ontario.

Just one day past her due date, on August 27, 2003, our little girl was born. She came into our lives in a wave of heat. It had been an extremely hot August. Her brothers were split on meeting this new being. Theo, being 5, was more understanding of the situation, and came down to see his new sister when she was only hours old. Zach was 3, and had been the baby. The baby who required a lot of Mama's time, so this would be an interesting adjustment for him.

Her birth story is one I always tell when given the opportunity. While I had hoped my last two baby births would be at home, neither had turned out that way. Mike was more than a little wary after our experience with Zach, so I conceded to a planned hospital birth with a midwife. My contractions started late in the evening on August 26. I can remember how uncomfortable I was having to travel in the car to get to the hospital. We knew that there was a possibility that we could get a birthing room that included a labour tub. We were told explicitly that 'birthing' should not happen in the tub. It was to be used only for labour. As luck would have it, we were given that room. I couldn't wait to get into a tub filled with warm soothing water, rushing around me like the bottom of a waterfall. The tub looked like a large recliner. If I recall correctly, I had to open a 'door' that swung open for me to enter the tub. Once closed and turned on, it would start to fill and slowly tilt to a horizontal position with the occupant gently immersed in the flowing warmth of water. Through each of my two previous labours, I had experienced excruciating back pain. I remember as Mike sat lovingly beside me, I dug my nails into his forearm to drive home the idea that this would be the last time I did this.

It didn't seem that much time had passed before I was telling my husband and midwife that I was sure it was time to push. The midwife disagreed, as it couldn't possibly be time for that. With closer inspection, she saw how right I was. I remember seeing my husband seemingly pinned against the wall, as we unsuccessfully tried to empty and right the tub. Suffice to say, Lauren came quickly, and I never made it to the bed. Within a few minutes, the two of us were swaddled in sheets and blankets. Her shock of black hair attested for the heartburn I had suffered over three months. We knew we would call her Lauren Rose. Her little smile was like the bud of her namesake. Our third and last child with us. By morning we were in our own bed, in our home dizzy and tired, with our newest addition. Theo made his way down to see his new sister. I don't think I will ever forget the love I saw that day.

I didn't want to put her down. I just wanted to hold this sweet little girl for the rest of her life. I don't think I had realized how much I had missed holding a newborn baby of my own making, without the cumbersome wires and IVs that attached to life-saving medications and monitors. I was grasping on to every moment of these early days, as I was now discovering that I had mourned this feeling when Zach was born. I didn't want anything or anybody to get in the way of bonding with my new baby girl. In these moments, I had this iron strong feeling that I should not let her go. I would reflect on the early days with Zach. To hold him was a choreographed manoeuvre designed with his life and safety in mind. I couldn't ever just pick him up and walk with him if he needed comforting. I couldn't bring him to my breast for nourishment and comfort anytime he needed it. I had to be aware of his heart rate, his oxygen level, his breathing rate at all times. Eventually, as Zach's condition improved over time, we found other ways to bond as mother and infant son. The feelings of grief came back as I found my way to bond with Lauren as mother and infant daughter. The fear was a surprise.

Someone had said to me once, in a conversation about having children, "Well we have 3, what's one more?" Well, I thought to myself, it's one more! Each new child brought with them an expansion of parental responsibility and care. A lifelong commitment to their well-being in every aspect that can be imagined. Theo was healthy, and thriving at three years old. Zach had had a rough start, but was a strong fighter. We still had to hyper-focus on all parts of his well-being, but he was a delight in every way.

Within a couple of years we had settled into a routine of young children, hospital and clinic. Theo was in grade one, Zach started JK, and little Lauren was a blessing. Supports for Zach continued through KidsAbility, and at school. He had frequent appointments for physiotherapy, occupational therapy, and speech therapy. Physically he struggled, but strength was coming. Every cold virus seemed to go straight to his lungs and manifest as pneumonia. This always meant a hospital stay with IV antibiotics. Many Christmases were spent tending the complications of a simple cold. He had many painful ear infections that would often put him in the hospital. Zach eventually needed a consult with an ear nose throat specialist at SickKids. During an appointment to assess his ears, the ENT noticed a split in Zach's uvula. Further investigation showed that he had a submucous cleft palate. This realization made sense as one of the speech issues that he had was a 'slushy' and 'nasal' quality. There was an increase of airflow when he made certain sounds, and now we knew why. This resulted in a referral to speech specialists at SickKids. Following tests and close investigation of Zach's mouth, it was suggested that an oral surgery called a z-plasty could be done. This would repair the cleft and possibly improve his speech. This was not an easy decision to make. We knew that it would be painful for him. We also knew that while this surgery seemed important for his speech development, in the grand picture, was it really necessary for him to endure a procedure like this that could put him at risk for infection? As I try to tug this memory off the high dusty shelf in my mind, I can remember how sore Zach was following the surgery. He already had some trouble eating enough to gain weight, now he had to contend with a very painful mouth. Thankfully, the hospital stay was short, and he recovered well. The procedure had been successful, and with time we would see if it had improved the quality of his speech.

As a mother with a busy family, I kept a calendar to keep track of all of our daily activities. Most families with more than one child will do the same. Days are dotted with deadlines for work, transporting to and from school, and extracurricular activities. Our calendar also held many time slots for medical check-ups. This is one of those memories that I am sure I suppressed until many years later. Things pile up at the best of times, and with so many life-challenging moments, we had accumulated boxes and boxes of things. In an attempt to finally gain back some space, a box housing my calendars was in front of me. Each book stamped with the year for which it tracked. It may seem to some that keeping these types of things is a silly space and time waster. Seeing these notes, these words written, the juxtaposition of the soccer practices against scheduled biopsies. This was not the vision of family that I had held. It was, however, the reality that we lived. The feeling that it would never end. That life would be this constant march of meds, appointments, food issues, procedures, poopy diapers, feeding tubes... trying to fit some sleep and laughter, and normalcy in there.

Lauren was spunky and determined from an early age. Strong and caring, an old soul who loved fiercely. Silly and serious, she could stand up to her brothers and her dad. We were revelling in all we had shouldered, and hopeful for a mediocre existence while we watched our children flourish in their maturing. Hopes and dreams. After Lauren was born, we didn't travel as a family again to Nova Scotia until many years later. When my niece Mary was getting married, Lauren and I flew down for the wedding. Lauren was not quite two years old at the time. It was wonderful spending the few days with family, young cousins playing together, laughing and giggling. It was a rare occasion to be together with my sisters and my mom. I dreamed that at some point I would be able to have my whole family travel with me to Nova Scotia again.

* * *

Regardless of what was happening in our lives, one thing remained. At least once a year, we would run in the rain. There always seemed to be a perfect temperature and perfect downfall. When Lauren was not yet a year old, Zach was almost 4 and Theo was almost 6, off we went. Out into the perfect downpour, laughing and running, Lauren in the sling, Zach on my other hip, and Theo running ahead. Splashing and kicking through the puddles, up and down the street. We were vaguely aware of some neighbours watching from their porches. I could feel their smiles.

* * *

I remember the day Zach started junior kindergarten at Tait Street Public School. I nearly made it through without crying, my heart beating faster than it should as I watched this tiny almost four-year-old walk into the school, following the others, crying pitifully while doing so. I thought my heart was breaking. How were we letting him walk into this new world full of new people? Little people who coughed and sneezed and slobbered. I was a bit of a mess that day. Unsure if we were doing the right thing. Zach would be attending morning classes every day, and come home at noon. Theo's schedule had been the same when he was in kindergarten. Half days, every day. Theo was now in grade one. In theory, it made sense, two kids to school in the morning, pick up one at noon, pick the other one up at 3:05pm. Sure I could do that. With a one-year-old in tow... alright, I guess that does make things a bit tricky. I was bound and bent to do this on my own, and to ensure that my kids got in some outdoor exercise at the same time. Whenever we were able, we walked the seven blocks to school. We had purchased a three-wheel double jogging stroller which made this trek so much easier. With Lauren in one side, and often Zach in the other, backpacks either stuffed in the undercarriage or thrown on top, we walked every day, rain, shine, snow or ice. These were wonderful days. I was being a mom, the way I wanted to be a mom. It was busy, exhausting and amazing all at once. We would still have to go to SickKids when necessary, but nothing like the days in the beginning. Zach still had nutritionist and physio appointments at the house. Due to his immunosuppression, we had to ensure that everyone was aware of the risks to him, being in kindergarten. One of those risks was the issue with chicken pox. I met with the principal, and drafted a letter that would go out to the kindergarten parents. This was the best way to ensure that if he needed the immunoglobulin shot following exposure, we could get it in the right time-frame. Our gratitude to humankind now extended to the many families who were understanding of our situation. Zach's life was now not only in our hands, but in the hands of our school community.

Zach adapted to going to school during that first year, but that doesn't mean it was an easy transition. He was very susceptible to any virus and bacteria that crossed his path. It was almost tradition that he would spend Christmas in the hospital with pneumonia. These instances were very commonplace to us now, and we all took them in stride. By April of 2005 Zach started to complain of being very tired. He was unable to climb the stairs, and was generally unhappy, and unwell. From April until June, Zach was in and out of hospital many times. He seemed to be getting progressively worse. There was no explanation for his deterioration, as far as a virus or bacteria. During an echocardiogram the technician asked me "What are they doing for Zachary's heart?" I was in no way prepared to answer this question, although deep down I seemed to know the answer. Later that day, the transplant team informed us of the truth about Zach's condition. He had what they called 'non-specific coronary artery disease.' In short, his body was rejecting his transplanted heart.

Shattered - 2005

We were shattered. We knew that a transplant was a trade-off. We knew that there would be complications, side effects. We certainly hadn't expected that a mere 4 years later Zach's heart would be failing. We were given a schedule of appointments to begin the process of putting Zach on the transplant list again.

In a daze, we fumbled through the end of June that year. A trip to Wonderland was planned. We needed to do something fun. Something to take our minds off the fact that our son's life was hanging in the balance. It was easy to find a campground fairly close to Wonderland. The plan was to drive to the head office for Mike's work to pick up the Wonderland tickets, then drive to Cold Creek Conservation Area to set up our camping spot for a couple of nights. This would place us just twenty minutes from Wonderland. We could spend a day enjoying the rides at the park, and have some camping time as well.

The day we were leaving, I was struggling with a stomach flu. I was barely able to take on ten minutes of preparation for this trip before I'd have to rest. I managed to get everything ready, dealing with our family of three kids under seven, and a dog. We were eventually able to get everything, including the kids, into the van. The trailer was hitched, we had all we needed for a couple of nights and we were putting our worry about Zach aside for the moment. An escape. Mike called to Sheila, who in my haste to get everything ready, I hadn't paid much attention to. It was unlike her to not already be in the van. She was a smart dog, and knew when a family trip was happening. She was usually the first in the van, but today she was lying in the shade in the yard. As Mike approached her, her head rose from her prone position and her tail moved feebly up and down. "Something's wrong with Sheila." Mike's voice cut through to my heart. Sheila was the first pet we had owned together.

The pain of loss that I saw on Mike's face washed over me. We had loaded Sheila into Mike's car. It had taken both of us to lift her. Her weight had seemingly doubled, and her abdomen was swollen and heavy. I waited in the van in our driveway with the kids while Mike drove Sheila to the vet. My mind was tracing over the last day to try and make sense of what had happened. I had been so busy the night before and all day, I hadn't really noticed that Sheila had not been underfoot. The night before, we had loaded some non-essentials in the van and ensured the trailer was ready to be hitched. We stood at the sidewalk chatting with neighbours, the kids running and playing close by on the lawn. Sheila was with us, her genetics as part border collie doing their job as she carefully stayed around the kids, corralling them as she saw fit to keep them safe. At one point she had spied a squirrel across the street. She took off like a shot, chasing the squirrel up the nearest tree. We called for her to return, and I remember saying, "That's likely the last time she'll run that fast." At the age of twelve, Sheila had certainly been slowing down. She had been with us since 1993 when we got her as a puppy.

As I reflected on that moment the night before, Mike returned from the vet. The kids were full of questions, but we could see the answer on his face. The veterinarian had explained that something had made an abdominal tumour burst. A sudden run could have done it. She was bleeding internally. Mike had returned without Sheila, after Dr. Doug had euthanized her. The weight of this loss now hung over us as we drove. We were trying to escape the sadness of our reality for a couple of days, and now the sadness had an additional layer.

We went through the motions of our plan. Trying to levitate the weekend for the kids. It was hard. They were feeling the loss of our sweet family pet as much as we were. The day that we went to Wonderland, Mike was suffering the twenty-four hour bug that had plagued me the day before. We hobbled through the park as best we could, going on the rides that the kids were enthused by, carrying Zach as we needed. As we were heading out of the park that day, Mike spied the Drop Tower. To my surprise he said, "I'm going on!!" This made little sense to me, as there was one sure thing I knew about my husband, and that was the fact that he didn't like heights. This ride, as the name implies, is a full-out drop once it has taken you two hundred and thirty feet into the air. Dutifully, as though there was no taking back his decision, Mike walked toward the ride and lined up. It wasn't long before he had taken his seat like everyone else, facing outwards, the safety yoke over his shoulders now gripped tightly in his hands. As the participants began the ascent to the top, Mike's crocs fell off his feet. Dear lord, he was going to shit his pants! I stood, hand shielding my eyes from the setting sun watching to be sure that he made it safely back, feet planted, albeit shakily, to the ground. When he returned, he said in a wobbly voice, "Why the hell did I do that? I hate heights!"

While it wasn't the trip we had hoped for, we made the best of it. To go back home meant facing what lay ahead of us. Once again, the unknown of waiting for a life-saving heart.

Another Heart

The process to put Zach on the waiting list required lots of visits and tests at SickKids. We managed his health the best we could, often needing to stay in the hospital. As his body rejected his heart, he was left feeling constantly tired. Climbing stairs was impossible due to the weakness and light-headedness. At any moment his condition could worsen.

The body is an amazing thing. A machine that runs often without us thinking about the incredibility of it. Each part of our body complements another so that we can grow, learn, move, walk, talk, and function. All of our faculties, our organs working together in harmony to keep us going. Zach had to be referred to nephrology soon after his first transplant. Dr. Harvey, the nephrologist, would joke that there was a standing argument between cardiologists and nephrologists as to which organ was more important; the heart or the kidneys. Each needed the other to survive, neither would do well if the other was failing. Zach's kidney function was showing signs of deterioration. So much so that it was thought that he might need a kidney transplant as well as a heart transplant. A biopsy was done in mid-July to hopefully rule out the need for a multiple organ transplant.

Zach's life had been rocky from the beginning. He always seemed to be hanging tenuously by a thread. I remember looking through his file at one point and reading the words "failure to thrive." These words had never been spoken by anyone to my ears. I sat and contemplated their meaning. His growth was never within the normal range. His weight was low, his size was low for his age. Those comparisons were made when looking at the numbers for a normal boy his age. Of course he wasn't hitting the charts the same way. His life had been anything but normal. Now, to ensure that he recovered well from another transplant, it was decided that he would need a gastronomy tube to help with nutrition. We had been through the stress of dealing with nasogastric tubes before, but the thought of putting a hole in Zach's abdomen was so traumatic. When we were told that Zach would need surgeries to repair his heart after he was born, I was absolutely terrified of the burden. What if I did something wrong in caring for him? That terror was maximized with the exchange of surgeries for a transplant. I felt ill-equipped to handle what Zachary would need from me. But I learned. I took notes. I read. I listened. I had to become a medical mom, knowing more about my child than the doctors did. I needed to be able to walk into a hospital at any time armoured with the knowledge that I knew he needed medical care before the doctors figured it out. I was proficient as a cardiac transplant mom, but now, I had to know how to care for a stoma and a g-tube too. I felt as though I were exploding.

The procedure for a g-tube insertion was done in the guided imaging lab. Zach would be sedated. Once the procedure was done, he'd have to stay admitted until he was well enough to go home. He had been admitted for a multitude of reasons just days before, with symptoms connected to his failing heart. At this point, we were to continue to monitor him at home, and his care now included medications for congestive heart failure, respiratory relief, and dietary restrictions to minimize the effort for his heart to pump.

By the end of July his name was on the list. We were told that he was still well enough to wait at home. A double-edged sword. This meant that finding a heart for him wasn't top priority. If a heart came in that was the right size and type, if there were another child waiting who was sicker than Zach, that child would get the heart. Of course.

That made perfect sense. Oh my god, the fact that there were other children waiting was completely heart-wrenching. How do you resolve these truths within yourself? For Zach to get a heart quickly, he needed to be sicker. What if he died while he was waiting? What if another child died while they were waiting in the hospital? Another child did have to die for Zach to live. Watching him deteriorate, again, was debilitating. All I could do was continue to care for him as he needed. Carry him when he was too tired. Lie next to him when he didn't have the energy to play. Laugh and cry with him. He was barely five years old. How must he be trying to understand what was happening?

We buckled down for the wait.

* * *

It was a regular August night. Zach had managed to stay at home over the past couple of weeks. Tonight he had the energy to ride his three-wheeler up and down the sidewalk. We were savouring the last weeks of summer holidays before school would start. I tried not to think too far ahead with the unknown of Zach's condition and fate still hanging, but at the same time, had to think about September and school for Theo. Tired from the day's activities, Zach, Lauren and Theo had fallen asleep with smiles, and I crawled into bed, falling asleep not long after a silent prayer. The phone woke me and I stumbled out, bleary-eyed and mindlessly annoyed that someone was calling in the middle of the night. It was Dr. Kantor. I felt myself pushing the phone into the side of my head. His voice was so very quiet as he told me that there was a heart for Zachary. He outlined our next steps as I strained to hear. Mike was now standing beside me rubbing his eyes, asking me what was happening.

Within an hour I had everything packed and ready. Now I had to wake Zach and explain that the heart we were waiting for would be at SickKids waiting for him. We had done our best to help him understand what was happening over the last few months. He was used to going to SickKids now. On a regular appointment day we would leave the house before six in the morning to arrive in time for blood work at eight. The drive was stressful, and when Zach was an infant it was highly traumatic. Now that he was five, it was slightly easier, and he would often fall back to sleep once he was buckled into his car seat. This morning, we were leaving at three o'clock. The drive was almost dream-like as the traffic at this early hour was practically non-existent. As I drove, I was in denial that this was happening. How could a heart be available for Zach so soon after being listed? Could this be real? Did we actually get a call at home? It seemed unheard of as usually those waiting in critical condition in hospital would receive life-saving organs first. Was Zach going to go into surgery just hours after riding his tricycle down the sidewalk?

We arrived at SickKids and went straight to the fourth floor. Zach was admitted to a room where we were to follow a list of pre-surgery preparations. First the nurse took all of his vitals. Zach was a pro at this, after having it done frequently over the last five years. After his vitals were taken, he was to have a bath with a special soap that would help to minimize any bacteria during the surgery. We methodically went through the list, bathing and getting into a hospital issue gown. Zach had not had anything to drink or eat since I had awakened him for our trip to the hospital. He would have to continue like this until after the transplant. On the outside I was the definition of calm. I had to be. On the inside I was falling apart with complete worry. This heart had failed him. This little heart that had grown with him since 2001 was struggling and would be replaced. Would he survive another transplant? Would I see Zach alive again? The fear wanted to consume me. I did what I could to keep it together.

Family Memories

Waiting again. The familiar room where I felt I had spent most of my life over the past five years. I would sit in silence. Thinking. Remembering. Trying to conjure up good memories.

* * *

As a family we continued to camp every summer until 2016. We had all of the camping gear needed to head off to the most beautiful spots. Theo was nine months old when he first came camping with us. For Zach and Lauren it would be the same. It was our family getaway each year. Eventually we bought a hard-top tent trailer to enjoy the provincial parks. I know there are many we could have visited. There were a couple that were favourites. Cyprus Lake on Georgian Bay is spectacular. The hike out to the Grotto is one we took many times. The kids thoroughly enjoyed the rocky trails. The cold water of the bay was not easy to get used to, but like a rite of passage we all took a quick dip. At night, the sky was as dark as black velvet, the stars pinpointing their sparkle. The milky way, a swath of glitter.

That first camping trip with Theo was to Cyprus Lake. Our little site was right on the edge of the lake itself. The sunlight on the water was peaceful and serene. The lake trail that connected to the Head of Trails was two steps from our site. That week holds memories that have wound their way into the fabric of family stories. The bulletin board at the camp office displayed a schedule of events. I noticed that we would be there for the annual Friends of the Bruce Pancake Breakfast. This sounded like a fabulous family outing! The breakfast would be hosted by a group of volunteers, in the park amphitheatre. Participants were to bring a plate, knife, fork, and cup along with them. The location, I decided, was close enough to hike to. What better way to start off your day, than a hike around the lake ended with a pancake breakfast cooked by volunteers? Theo would need to travel in the back-pack carrier. Mike was less than enthusiastic about the whole idea. Why would I want to walk anywhere for breakfast? he queried more than once. I hoped that his tone would change once in the midst of the experience. The walk and breakfast were all I hoped they would be. A lovely morning, the path still wet with dew. Just enough chill in the air to remind you that autumn was around the corner. The sun's rays teasing a glimpse of the warmth it would provide as the day went on. We arrived at the amphitheatre to find many campers lined up to enjoy their breakfast. The volunteers moved the line through swiftly as each person received pancakes, bacon, sausages, and syrup. Our cups were filled with coffee, tea or juice, and we were sent off to find a spot to eat along the seats of the outdoor theatre. I was aware of a warm sense of community in this moment. Sitting with my husband and my son. Simple, yet so important. Mike was not a happy camper, however. He didn't fancy having to wait in line for his coffee. He didn't really complain too much, but when he did speak it was clear he didn't share my sentiments of this outing. I was a little saddened that I had pushed this horrible experience on him. The funny part of this story would eventually come out years later. At some point, during a social gathering, the topic of camping had come up, and many of us were sharing camping stories. Mike began to tell the story of our hike to the pancake breakfast, and how much he enjoyed it. I imagine my jaw was on the floor. For so many years I thought he had despised it. Yet here he was regaling everyone with the joys of this little family outing.

Suffice to say, I have learned that it takes Mike a long time to warm up to things. So long in fact, I might not know he's warmed until years later.

Surprising Recovery

At some point I was brought back to reality by the surgeon, Dr. Calderone, coming in to let me know that Zach was in recovery. I was already anticipating months in the hospital and was preparing myself and Zach for the long days ahead. To my surprise, his post-surgery time in CCU was very short. He was awake and extubated by one-thirty in the morning, August 7th, and was eating freezies. By the eighth he was moved to the cardiac floor. When Zach had his first transplant, the cardiac wing on the fourth floor was where children waited for their life-saving hearts. Following transplant, they would go to the sixth floor to the multi-transplant wing. The doctors and nurses there were trained to care for children who had received any organ through transplant. It was a strange transition, not knowing any of the nurses, and realizing that they may not know the intricacies of your child. Four years later, that had changed. Cardiac transplant children were now brought to the fourth floor cardiac inpatient wing, where their care was completely tailored to their needs as a transplant patient as well as a cardiac patient.

Zach was in the step-down room, a room with space for four patients and nurses in the room at all times. It was incredible for him to be doing so well at this point. Such a contrast from the first transplant experience. There had been no need to keep him sedated and muscle-relaxed like before. Three days post transplant he was sitting on my lap. His new g-tube was being used to ensure his nutrition intake, and he was being motivated to eat regularly.

I was told he needed to stay in the hospital for at least a week, moving from the step-down room to a private room before being discharged. This all happened very quickly. During the few days in step-down, Zach recovered well physically, having chest tubes removed, x-rays to look at his heart and lungs, as well as an echo to check on how this new heart looked. Zach, however, was showing me that he was not happy. He had always been one to wear his emotions on his sleeve. He rarely hid how he was feeling, and this experience was no different. With any attempt on my part to engage with him, I was met with a big-eyed, sad stare and then avoidance. Zach didn't speak to me for at least three days. It was heart-breaking. There had been so many times in his life when I had wanted to take on his pain. Wanted to put myself in his place to absorb all of the physical and emotional struggle of what he had and would endure. Each night, I would kiss him and snuggle him as he lay in his hospital bed, and then have to leave. In a step-down room there was no space for a parent to stay. Any parent rooms in the hospital were occupied by those who were awaiting news of their child's well-being following a surgery. I was not able to stay.

I would leave at night, get on the subway and travel to Mary's apartment about half an hour away. She and her husband Dre lived in the city, and we often used an appointment at SickKids as a reason to visit with them. Each morning I would head back to the hospital from their place as early as I could, to spend the day with Zach and hope that he would talk to me.

He broke his silence on August 11th. He had been eating fairly well, but on this morning he insisted that he have some French toast. When we inquired, we were told that due to his dietary issues, they couldn't give him French toast because it contained milk. He was not budging on this one, and unfortunately there was nothing that could be done. Food had to be ordered for each patient following any specific dietary specifications, and one of Zach's was that he had an intolerance to lactose. At home, I would make French toast with bread and egg. No milk required. Here, they would only make it one way; with milk mixed in the egg. I went off on a mission, trying to figure out how to get this boy his French toast. This desire is what had prompted him to talk, I needed to reward that with what he was craving. I went down to the atrium food court and walked into the Terrace Cafe looking for options. There was only one station that offered French toast. They made it with milk. While the Terrace Cafe may look like a food court to the outsiders, behind each station was a large shared work area where all of the food was prepped. The French toast from the patient menu was made right here. How was I going to get this breakfast for my Zach? I scanned the menu again, and a line was now forming behind me. I saw an option on the menu; 1 egg any way. I told the cook that I had a son upstairs who had just had a transplant, and he wanted French toast, and he was going to make it for me. I said, "Take a piece of bread. Now, take an egg. Crack it in a bowl and mix it with a fork. Now take that piece of bread and coat it with the egg and put the coated bread on the grill. Flip it over once brown on one side. There. That's how I want an egg." The cook looked at me sideways. The people in line after me stifled laughter behind their smiles. I don't know if there has ever been a piece of French toast any better made than that piece was.

A week after his transplant, Zach was well enough to move to the private room, where he would continue to recover and we would learn anything necessary to take him home safely. By now we were seasoned transplant parents, so this was pretty easy to navigate. What had me reeling was the speed at which he was recovering, and with few complications. Certainly nothing like what he had experienced four years ago.

I could now stay in the room with Zach, and called home with a list of things that I would need to make the stay more comfortable. Barry and Linda had come up to help Mike at home with Theo and Lauren. I was still anticipating at least three or four days before Zach would be given his discharge papers, but I couldn't believe it when just two nights after moving to his private room we were sent home! Zach's recovery was nothing short of amazing, and his resiliency still amazes everyone. He couldn't wait to be home, playing with his brother and sister, and meeting new friends who had moved to the neighbourhood.

There were still a lot of follow-up appointments, and lots of in-house care to be done, including nutrition, physiotherapy, and occupational therapy. This, however, was all very usual for us, and we quickly set into a routine.

Disney

The idea of a wish trip was almost unfathomable. A trip like this would take so much time to plan, yet here we were, on a plane, all five of us heading to Orlando from Toronto. It had been mentioned a couple of times, when Zach and I were in the clinic, that we should be getting an application from our social worker to apply for a Wish for Zach. By late 2006 we felt confident that Zach was well enough to go on a trip. Disney was a big favourite, so we opted for the package that Children's Wish provided. The accommodations were beautiful, with many amenities on site. We were provided with a rental vehicle to travel in, and had a packed itinerary for the week.

Each day was a new adventure, with passes to Disney for three days, Universal Studios for one day, and Marineland for one day. This left two travel days, one on either end of the week, for flying in and flying home. We were exhausted by the end of every day, falling into bed with smiles and memories to take with us. We either had fast passes to forego the long waits, or utilized the Children's Wish T-shirts we had been given to ensure that we got the maximum experience. The park staff were amazing in helping us with that whenever they could.

On one of the nights at Disney, Mike insisted that he take Zach and Theo on the Tower of Terror. Lauren and I waited below and munched on turkey legs. After the ride, Mike walked over with the boys, all of them giggling. Mike told us how they had stood on the ride waiting in anticipation for each jump and scare. Zach, as usual, was holding his half-zip zipper pull between his teeth. When they came out of the ride, Mike looked at Zach just as he was dropping the bitten off zipper pull into his hand from his mouth. He had bitten clean through the rubber pull during the ride!

A New Home

Our little home on Tait Street was feeling cramped and small as our children grew. We needed more space, that would only be attained by making a move. We had contemplated renovations and additions to the house, but the property space just didn't support this avenue. As we searched the city for a new home, I agonized over leaving our little community. It was important to me that our children continued to go to the same school that they started their educational careers in. Perhaps a holdover from my own childhood, I didn't want them to have to change schools. I had become rooted in our community, and didn't really want to move outside of it. Mike was more open-minded about this. He was happy to look further afield than I was. I agreed that if we did move to a different area within Cambridge, our children would be fine. They were resilient and would adapt to the change. However, something to me was important about staying within our built-up support system. We eventually found a house still within our neighbourhood. The house would offer more space, a nice yard, close to a park and still within the same school catchment area.

Moving day was crazy! It was one of the hottest days ever for the month of June. There were many difficulties that day, but we made it in, ensured each room had a mattress and sheets for sleeping, and fell into exhausted rest after the long day. Staying within the community kept us connected to our friends, and our children's friends.

Another Sister

Early in our relationship, before we were engaged, Mike confided in me that he had a daughter. Sarah had been born before we met, and had not been a part of his life at that point. After we married, and Sarah had grown into adulthood, she reached out to connect with her dad. Following a couple of awkward yet positive connections between Mike and Sarah, we invited her to come visit us and meet the rest of her family. When we told the kids about their older sister, they were thrilled! The idea of having another sibling was exciting to them. This was the beginning of a beautiful connection, and some healing for Mike. It wasn't always easy as past hurts were often uncovered and discussed. Sarah joined us often for holidays, family camping trips and vacations. In retrospect, it seems that she has always been with us, a very important part of our family. Having Sarah with us, our family felt whole.

Stanley Street Hockey

You don't need much to start a hockey game. Perhaps it's a photograph, or maybe just a memory. I can see Mike in the driveway with Zach and Theo. The boys are wearing hand-knit sweaters to keep them warm on the chill day in October. It was Thanksgiving. I had put a turkey in the oven, and we decided to go for a trail walk just outside of town while the turkey roasted. When we returned, Dad got a couple of hockey sticks and a ball out of the garage, and was showing Theo and Zach how to stick-handle the ball. This was the beginning of a long-standing community activity. Whether it was this particular day, or the next day; what I remember is this: A small pickup game was started. Mike and the boys discovered another dad with his kids just down the street, who were also out with their sticks and balls. They laughed and had fun that day. The next Sunday, they were out playing again, and thus it began. Whether it was spoken or not, each Sunday after that, they would meet on our little street and play a game of hockey. The teams slowly grew. But the weather didn't cooperate for long. Eventually, the ice and snow put the street to sleep for the winter. The next fall, though, we all knew that Sunday was Road Hockey Day on Stanley Street. The players were young and old alike, regardless of gender. The teams were a mixed bag. Each year the participant list grew. It was actually turning into an organized seasonal event. At one point there were at least four teams, and sometimes two games being played at once. Specific rules were made for the little hockey league that was created. The number of games per season was determined, and at the end? A tournament! A Stanley Street Cup was the coveted trophy! Awards for Most Improved, Best Kid Player, Best Dad Player... something for everyone.

The tournament ended with a tailgate feast, burgers, chili, treats, and a cake. This tradition continues to this day.

All three of our kids at some point enjoyed these road hockey games. It was also a great spectator sport that brought the small community together each week. The kids recruited new players each year, spreading the word. It was not uncommon for someone to be walking by, see the games being played and ask if they could join in. Oftentimes, these players would come back week after week. Sometimes there were players who would drive from out of town to come and play. These were the glory days. Over time, kids grew up, people moved to new neighbourhoods. Some families continue to play each year. It's a smaller core group, still fun for those who continue. New families have moved to Stanley Street, and the teams continue to have a mix of dads, moms, and boys and girls of all ages.

Friends Are Family

Our kids all adored Peggy and Tad. As often happens, our paths at some point began to drift, but then were drawn together again. We made sure that we visited with them more than a few times each year. Once when Mike and I had been invited to a wedding in Toronto, Peggy and Tad stayed with the kids in our home so that we could go for the night. Following that, we decided that they would be the right pick as guardians for Theo, Zach and Lauren if anything ever happened to Mike and me. We loved spending time with them for Easter and Thanksgiving dinners, as they invited us into their family gatherings on these occasions for many years.

We would often go to their place for a barbecue or dinner, and spend the evening watching a hockey game, screaming at the television for the Leafs to win, or the Wii would come out and rousing games of Mario Kart, Bowling, Guitar Hero or Rock Band were played by all.

Vacation - All I Ever Wanted

Our family camping trips continued, oftentimes including visits to friends or family across the province as we towed our gear and trailer around. When Zach was little, it was less than easy to manage his health needs while camping, but the positive outweighed the negative. For us, these trips were family bonding at its best. Theo would perfect a method of making s'mores that he was always proud to demonstrate.

One summer, my niece in Nova Scotia was getting married. While I would have loved for our family to travel east for the wedding, it simply wasn't affordable. Mike decided that while I was away, he would take the kids and the trailer to a local family run campground. A few of his workmates had seasonal sites there. I believe the kids would have been seven, five and three at the time. I came home to hear all of the stories from the kids about camping with Dad. The funniest yet is how Lauren woke her dad up one of those mornings. After a few attempts to wake him up, shaking him and calling "Dad, Dad, it's time to get up," she was unsuccessful. Dad just wasn't ready to wake. The next thing Mike knew, he felt little fingers prying his eyelids open. Right in front of his eye was his own watch being held within inches of his face. "Dad! It's time to get up!!" Lauren was not subtle. When she had a point to get across, she was determined. We laugh to this day about her methods.

Our favourite spots were right here in Ontario. I remember the first time we had hiked out to the Grotto. I turned to Mike and wondered aloud, why did anyone go elsewhere for beautiful vistas.? One year we ventured to a closer spot, and went south instead of north. We set up our trailer and gear at Turkey Point Provincial Park for a week. Within an hour, we started to realize that we recognized three children who had biked past our site many times. We watched and followed them back to their site, and were pleasantly surprised to find our neighbours from Cambridge! This was exciting for the kids to be camping so close. They had a wonderful time vacationing together, which started a camping tradition that we participated in for at least three years. Some of Mike's high school friends would join us on many of these trips, either to Turkey Point or to Port Burwell.

Drawing Hope

I t seemed unbelievable in so many ways that Zach would be going into middle school. We had navigated his elementary school years, at times it seemed, by the skin of our teeth. Zach had an amazing group of friends who cared about him. All we could do was continue to provide him with a solid home life and love to carry him through. We had never opted for organ transplantation as a means to keep him in a bubble, never to understand the joy of living life. As frightening as it often was, we balanced the risks against the experiences. Isn't that what parenting ultimately is? Always and forever weighing each moment for risk and rewards. For someone like Zach the balance was trickier. The risks could be hiding within a simple connection. A cough, a sneeze... And here he was moving into a new arena. Out of a comfort zone that had held him, held us for eight years of his educational career.

Zach had an amazing teacher for his seventh grade. He was doing as well as he could be and loving life. He continued on to the eighth grade without much fanfare. Honestly, a mediocre life is all I could ever hope for. Late in 2013, we were contacted by a fellow heart transplant mom. She had been in contact with an amazing photographer who was working on an incredible project. Shawn had begun a photo project that connected him to children who were living with serious health conditions. He had already done a photo for Joanna's daughter as well as a few other kids. NBC wanted to do a piece on him for their upcoming One Day One Deed segment airing in April of 2014. Joanna thought that Zach's story would be perfect for Shawn and for NBC. By April of 2014, everything was in place, and we were ready for an NBC crew, along with Shawn Van Daele to come into our lives. Zach's homework had been to draw himself picturing what he hoped for his future. We reached out to Zach's art teacher at school to help him with his ideas. The result was a picture of Zach opening his own Quesadilla shop and winning the Stanley Cup with his beloved Toronto Maple Leafs! The photoshoot and interview with NBC went off without a hitch. Shawn worked his magic, returning the next day with the completed and framed photo. This amazing experience has resulted in a long lasting connection with Shawn, and beautiful inspiration that your hopes and dreams regardless of what obstacles you might face can be possible.

Never the Same - 2016

Days trudged onward, collecting, seemingly without my knowledge, into a grouping of weeks and months... even years. Things for Zach progressively got better, fewer visits to SickKids, less hospitalizations. Our family seemed to be settling into a wonderful feeling of normalcy. As Mike's career in insurance made some headway, I focused on working on a college diploma in ECE. Zach had started high school, something we thought might never happen. Theo made his way through elementary school and into middle school with a smile. That kid woke up happy. Almost simultaneously, his eyes would open and a smile would span his mouth. No doubt that a large part of his character was shaped by the time we had spent in Toronto with Zach at SickKids. He had a sense of caring and compassion that drew people to him. He had to have his tonsils removed while he was in the first grade, following a number of incidences of strep throat. While he was in the seventh and eighth grade he was often calling to come home from school due to bad sinus headaches. When he was about seventeen, allergies started to develop. He found out that he was quite allergic to horses, as well as cats and dogs. This was not something that I was familiar with, but his dad had dealt with asthma, and his uncles and aunt on this side of the family had allergies as well. It was a learning curve for Theo and for me to learn to manage this. He was consistently dealing with congestion and headaches. Eventually, he did seem to find what worked best to control his symptoms and exposures.

On Christmas Eve 2015 Zach, Lauren and I went shopping for a few last items. We had stopped at a local coffee shop and picked up something to eat on the way. We hadn't spent much time in the store, but I could tell Lauren needed to sit down. I watched her as I stood in line at the cashier. She looked as though she would fall any moment. I was able to get through the line, and get to her side, just as she slumped into my arms. I held her up, frantic as she was clammy and pale. She responded to me, and said she felt as though she needed to get to a washroom. We made our way through the store to the washrooms and waited for what seemed an eternity for vacancy. By this time, Lauren was feeling a bit better. We chalked her episode up to being tired, and overheated due to her new winter coat.

As I neared the last couple of months of my final semester, Lauren continued to display non-specific symptoms of joint pain, and another fainting episode.

Battery of Tests - 2016

Following the extensive history-taking by the nurse practitioner, some blood was taken. The doctor then joined us, and went over the history. She said that she wanted Lauren to be seen by the ENT down the hall. He would examine the swelling on Lauren's face. The MRI that had been done in Cambridge showed the mass. It was in the bone and tissue. Outwardly, the swelling seemed to be in her cheekbone. Physiologically, it was in her mandible, so having an ear nose throat specialist look at her made sense. That day I watched my daughter endure very difficult situations. Parents have hopes and dreams for their children, and we also carry worry. When they come to the age of adolescence we worry about how they will navigate social situations. How will they handle the things that life will throw at them? I know that I wasn't prepared for this day. Had we equipped Lauren with the ability to handle what was to come? My love and admiration for my daughter's strength of character and courage grew tenfold that day. I sat and watched as Lauren took needles in her mouth and allowed a biopsy to be done on the growth that was found in her jaw. The doctor motioned to Mike and me to come and look in her mouth, where we were shocked to see the asymmetry of her upper jaw. The left side had expanded to three times its size. That is where the growth was. The doctor had taken a needle, and withdrew sections of the growth for analysis.

I was speechless and foggy. I couldn't believe what was happening, and the day had just begun. When we had entered the hospital, both Mike and I felt the sudden feeling of being pushed again towards the precipice. This time, the hospital was different. This time it was another of our beloved children. Hadn't we been through enough with Zach?

We were sent back to the oncology clinic. Each trip through these unfamiliar halls seemed to be solidifying a future. A future that no one would ever want for their child. The clinic staff quickly sent us for the next tests they needed. A CT scan and x-rays were ordered. They were looking for other lumps. Blood work that had been done was inconclusive, and the chest x-ray was fine. We were sent to the fracture clinic to see Dr. Burrows. The x-ray of Lauren's wrist showed a possible fracture or buckle of a small bone. Dr. Burrows examined the x-ray and felt that there was no fracture; however, she thought that the pain was probably related to another health issue. We traipsed back to the oncology clinic, where we were told to go home and call on Monday for results. At this point, it didn't seem to be a question of 'was it cancer or not?' It was a question of what kind of cancer. Cancer. The dreaded 'C' word. Was it leukemia or lymphoma?

On March 7, Lauren and I sat on the couch after waking. The day was as grey as our mood. We tried to keep things light, but the unknowing surrounded us like a fog. As we talked, Lauren was scratching her head. As she did so, she noticed a lump... and then 2 more. I called McMaster for the results of the tests that had been done the week before. The biopsy of the mass in Lauren's mandible was inconclusive. The CT scan showed 3 other lumps forming on her scalp, and there were spots on her liver. To fully determine the true diagnosis a bone marrow aspiration would be done, as well as a second biopsy of the growth in her mandible. We were to arrive the next morning for these tests. It was very hard not to look for answers myself. I would search online, trying my best to leave my emotions out of my findings. What would be worse? Would knowing be worse than our ignorance? If only we could lock ourselves away. To never have to hear the truth. Surely this logic would work. If we didn't know, it wouldn't be true.

We were very familiar with heart catheterizations and biopsies with Zach. We had no idea what to expect with a bone marrow biopsy. We arrived early at McMaster and went straight to 'finger poke.' The room was tucked back in behind the imaging department, and surgical waiting room. In order for oncology patients to have timely blood results, a small room and waiting area were created just inside the blood lab. This would be the first of many visits here. We were greeted by Nate, a child-life worker whom we would come to know well. Here Lauren sat and warmed her finger, and then had a lab tech take enough blood from a finger poke to fill many small vials. Following finger poke we made our way to the 3F clinic again. We were greeted by Cheryl at the desk. She smiled and told us not to worry, that she would get to know our names soon, as she found Lauren's clinic sheet and name band in her stack. I wanted to say, "Like hell you will." Deep down I seemed to know she was right. To prepare for the procedure, Lauren had to fast from the night before. An IV was put in and we waited for her to be called in for her bone marrow aspiration. The clinic was very busy that day. It was a storm of noise and people. So many families. Children were sitting at small tables doing crafts and laughing. Others were in the midst of IV treatments. Soon it was time for Lauren to go. We were walked to the sedation clinic, and led to a stretcher. Lauren was met by Christine, the child life worker. She spoke with Lauren and us, and asked questions about what she might be able to do to help put Lauren at ease. Lauren was brave and quiet. In the procedure room, Kevin the anesthesiologist nurse practitioner looked at Lauren's hospital name bracelet and asked her about the blue bracelet that was next to it. Lauren told him about her trip to Ripley's and her bet with her friend Chloe to see who could keep their bracelet on the longest. The whole crew laughed at this and were so keen on Lauren's story of her trip to Ripley's and how she had slept in the shark tunnel the past weekend with her Pathfinder's group. Lauren was hooked up to a monitor, and blood pressure, then given sedation medicine. As she drifted off, Mike and I were ushered out of the room. Right around the corner from the sedation room within the lab were the recovery bays. We were shown where Lauren would be brought to recover, and we sat to wait. We were prepared for a lengthy wait, as Zach's procedures typically took at least an hour before he was taken to recovery. Within fifteen minutes, Lauren was brought out. We were surprised at how quickly the procedure was done. Lauren needed some morphine for pain as she woke from the daze of sedation. Once she was awake, she was discharged and we went home. It was a quiet and difficult drive. It was uncomfortable for Lauren to sit following her procedure. All we could do was hope and pray that all the tests were wrong. We wanted desperately for the professionals to have made mistakes on this one.

The next day the phone rang and the news was received. No amount of hope and prayer would change what we were told. Lauren would need to be admitted. I drew my girl in towards me for a hug, and we wept. All we knew at this point was that it was leukemia. We were to meet with Dr. Breaky in the 3F clinic that day to discuss the diagnosis and the plan for treatment.

We went through the task of packing to go to the hospital. I had called Mike to break the news to him. I don't remember what the weather was like. My heart and soul were in a stormy turmoil, emotion upheaving my being like waves crashing the shore relentlessly.

Quickly following diagnosis, we were plunged into a crash course in cancer. We were told that Lauren had acute lymphoblastic leukemia, and that she would require chemotherapy. Her oncologist was encouraging. Her diagnosis included the phrase, "high risk." This was apparently a good thing, as the alternative was "very high risk." How reassuring. Truly. Yet somehow still very frightening.

With our growing experience with medical professionals, we knew that their perspective was very different from a parent's. While the intent is of course to alleviate fear of loss, it doesn't quite translate when one is hearing the news that one's child has a critical illness and requires extensive and invasive treatment to survive.

Lauren and I moved into a ward room on 3B at McMaster. Lauren was hooked up to another IV and started on Allopurinol to prevent build-up of uric acid during chemotherapy. Once the drugs start to kill the cancer, the dying leukemia cells create a build-up of uric acid which crystallizes in the kidneys. The next day Lauren went for an ECHO to get a baseline of her heart function before the chemo was to be started. Another MRI was also scheduled for that afternoon to get a better look at the lumps on her head. A lumbar puncture was to be done after that to inject a chemotherapy drug into her spinal fluid.

Support From Far and Wide

We were being raised up by many wonderful people in our lives. At a time when we were feeling as though our world was shattering, we had support pouring in for Lauren and our family that was truly healing. It was difficult to find words to express the deep gratitude and profound meaning that this had. The messages of love and support, gifts of meals for the family, coordination of funds, people working together... was all working to provide us with the strength and courage we needed to beat this cancer with Lauren. As a family we did our best to remain strong to get through with the help from many family and friends.

By March 20, 2016 Lauren had had her first chemo. At this point she was tolerating it fairly well. She was brave and positive. Lauren chose a mantra for her journey; ***Believe***. She believed that she would beat this. We had to believe that she could bear it. Positive words and thoughts have healing power. We took courage in the knowledge that family and friends had also battled and beat cancer.

Despite all the support, we knew that this fight had just begun. We still felt shell-shocked. Regardless of the perceived ease in which Lauren had tolerated her chemo to this point, we knew that the side effects would be difficult in weeks to come. We persevered; we took each day as it presented itself.

Lauren was discharged from the oncology ward within a couple of weeks, and would receive her next chemo treatments as an outpatient. Some of these treatments would require overnight stays in hospital. We would have to travel to McMaster at least weekly. When the chemo rendered her body unable to fight infection, she would have to be admitted again.

Inspiration was coming to us through the knowledge that so many cancer warriors have gone before her into this battle and emerged on the other side. Inspiration was coming to us every day through the messages sent, the food that came to the door, the phone calls, cards and packages filled with love. We appreciated all the support and positivity. We continued to be genuinely touched and awed by the outpouring of help.

After a month into this journey Lauren experienced some twists and turns. She was to have a couple of routine procedures one day, but side effects from chemotherapy treatment put up a roadblock. It is frightening seeing the side effects of these treatment drugs. While the chemotherapy gets rid of the monster that cancer is, it beats down and weakens the body. The body's defences are battered and cannot fight off the simplest of infections. This means that often the best care is in hospital. She was back in hospital at McMaster for a few days. At times our spirits were low. Spending time in the hospital was exhausting and difficult for the whole family. Lauren's spirits and overall well-being were better after some antibiotics and a transfusion. Lauren's days were brightened by the love received by way of inquiries, messages, mail, meals, and gifts. It all helped her to Believe.

On April 14th, 2016 the results from Lauren's bone marrow aspiration that had been taken the previous Tuesday showed that she was in remission!! She would still need further chemotherapy, starting next week with a more intensive schedule. When the words "Lauren is in remission" gently flowed from Dr. Portwine's mouth, it was a bittersweet moment. If only it meant that the treatments were done. If only it meant that we could pack up and go home and forget that this had ever happened. Instead we knew all too well that the treatment would continue. The drugs used to eradicate the cancer cells in her bone marrow had to continue to be administered through many other phases before she was done. The beast could come back without warning so the war was still on. We were happy to be going home to enjoy some time with family before the next step.

With the first battle of Lauren's cancer war won, the next phase was looming. To ensure that it wouldn't come back, Lauren was in for 2 years and 3 months of chemotherapy. We were to go back to McMaster for 2 weeks of inpatient treatment. Different drugs, different schedules, more side effects. Each day was to be taken as it presented, and we had to deal with its challenges. Mostly tired, often achy, sometimes annoyed; Lauren was still Lauren. This war would change her. It would change us, but we wouldn't let it take the best of us. She had cancer, but cancer didn't have her. Onward we would go.

As a mom, you never want to see your children suffering. Every illness that keeps them from being themselves is a heartache. You want to be able to take away the fevers, the upset, the fatigue.... With this war comes the risk of infection. By April 26, Lauren had been running fevers for well over a week and a half. The team at the hospital were doing everything they could to make her comfortable, treating the symptoms, and investigating the source. Finally an answer was discovered. She had picked up noro-virus somewhere, and of course with her suppressed immune system couldn't fight it off. There was nothing to do but let it run its course. By all accounts, her symptoms really could have been worse, but she was still too sick to be out of the hospital. It was a setback; we faced it and moved forward. Chemo still continued. We had so many sending thoughts and prayers to help boost our belief that the end to this war would be a win for Lauren.

By the next day, Lauren had been more than 24 hours without fever. They were happy to let her leave for the day, so we went to

Ronald McDonald House until bedtime. It looked like she had kicked the virus! We hoped to be discharged within a couple of days.

After a couple of weeks, the pattern of chemotherapy changed according to the protocol. What had been weekly chemo in-clinic would now be daily and we would stay at RMH to ease the burden of her treatments. This made it difficult for our family, as we would be apart. We chose to dwell on the best moments as we counted down the days of what looked to be a very long journey. Lumbar punctures with chemo continued during this time, as well as IV chemo. The usual side effects occurred making Lauren feel exhausted and sick to her stomach. She and I fell into the routine of being at McMaster and RMH through the week and then home on the weekends. We tried to fill our days with moments to remember, aside from her feeling tired and nauseated. Lauren endured this through until the end of June.

Lauren and I were back at McMaster for the last week of this phase. We had to wait for the results of her blood work to confirm that her numbers were within the parameters to start the next round of chemo. If her counts were good, she was there for the week. The first 2 days would be busy with MRIs, lumbar puncture and bone marrow samples. The infusion of 24-hour chemo would start, and then once her blood work showed her system was clearing the drug, we could go home. Each new phase brought its own difficulties. It was important for her to drink lots of fluids during this infusion, and she would also be flushed through with saline to move this nasty drug out of her system. This meant lots of trips to the washroom as the drug cleared. But the washroom was down the hall. Sometimes we would get a portable commode in her room to make it easier. Moving through the hallways with an IV pole while feeling completely drained is not the easiest of tasks. The washroom needs continue, regardless of whether or not your body needs to sleep.

We knew it would be a long week. This next phase of treatment would take us through the summer. This journey was taking its toll on all of us. Having to be away from family and our home was difficult to say the least. We knew that there was a long road ahead; we would strive to take one day at a time, and for the most part we were doing all right. When all possibilities were considered, I knew that things could be worse. We had seen and met children here who were struggling more than Lauren was with the side effects of the drugs.

I did often wish, however, that one morning I would wake to find it had all been a nightmare and we were as before. I would go to Lauren's room to see her sleeping there looking as she did before this all came crashing down.

I looked at her now, sleeping, and was moved by the strength she showed during this time of profound vulnerability. I am proud of her character, her sensibility, and her ability to persevere. I love her. She is a bright and shining light.

As the summer weeks were coming to a close, the days in September still held the heat of the season. Lauren was soon to start a different phase of her chemo called delayed intensification. A phase that would last about seven weeks. I felt like an office manager, managing the business of cancer for my daughter. It was my duty to keep track of the schedule, know the drugs and their possible side effects, ensure that she was getting them, the right drugs, at the right dose at the right time every day. Some had to be taken on an empty stomach, some had to be taken with food. Some made her feel sick to her stomach. Side effects were not only the usual ones that we all hear about, but others like nerve damage that leads to loss of feeling in fingertips and toes. The inability to lift your feet properly, called foot drop, increases the possibility of dangerous trips and falls. Lauren was diagnosed with foot-drop during the summer months, and was assessed for the need of orthotics. She was pleased to have this assessment, and was happy to be able to design these new helpers. She chose a very unique mix of hearts, roses and batman. Lauren, with her quiet charm, made quick friends with her orthotics assessor. Once she got the orthotics in October, it made such a difference for her. She had also started to take a cocktail of vitamins at the suggestion of Dr. Tarnopolsky, a neurologist, to possibly assist in the regeneration of her nerve damage from the Vincristine. The drug, while hopefully ensuring that leukemia will not return, caused neuropathy or nerve damage that inhibited Lauren's ability to walk safely. This cocktail was four different pills taken twice a day. These were not the easiest pills to take, but she took them knowing that it increased her chances of having some part of her independence back.

On September 13th, we were devastated and struggled with the news that the first family we met on our journey with Lauren's cancer were experiencing the loss of their daughter. Valerie Sommer and her daughter Claire were our first roommates at McMaster. Lauren and Claire had the opportunity to do some crafts together, and Valerie provided a smiling face and support during such an uncertain time. We had kept in contact since then, and were deeply sorrowed by Claire's passing. Claire had given Lauren flowered letters that she had made, and Lauren treasured them.

Attending Claire's funeral was very emotional. We were so saddened by the reality of a life taken too soon by childhood cancer. I had been unsure about sharing this day with Lauren. How do you help your child deal with the death of someone she knew for only a short time, but who had been through the same hospital stays and treatments? Lauren understood that Claire's cancer was very different from hers. This was how Lauren coped with this profound knowledge, the understanding that her diagnosis and prognosis were different. She had to cling to this. This would not be the only time we would face loss like this.

Days and weeks seemed to blend into one another. We were now counting down to the end of this phase so that Lauren could start the final portion of this nasty journey. Maintenance promised to be the easiest part, albeit the longest. We heard heartening stories from the nurses and other families that she'd feel so much better while on maintenance, and be able to do so much more. Right now though, it was next week, the week after, the week after... more chemo. Lauren had homeschooling for the beginning of her eighth grade year. A lovely teacher by the name of Karen would come to our home 3 days a week as long as Lauren felt up to it, to help in her English and Math classes.

Childhood cancer threatens the child's right to a childhood filled with happiness, laughter and learning, yet these children still smile. The drugs and their side effects wreak havoc on their bodies and their psyches. Yet many still smile. These children must often face their own mortality and that of their peers, well before they should have to. Yet somehow I still see their smiles.

We stayed positive. We knew that Lauren's journey had been relatively easy, considering the possibilities.

I tell you all of this to raise awareness. Too many children have to endure this horrendously devastating disease.

Be aware. Childhood cancer affects too many. More research is needed. Funding is required so that agencies can continue to provide important support. Not all families have a large network of family and friends to fall back on.

By October 2, 2016 Lauren had endured almost 7 months of chemotherapy. That was only 7 months of the total 27 months of treatment; 20 months of treatment to go. Yes, the treatments would be less invasive, yes, she was home more than in hospital. Yes, she was lucky. Lucky that some of the side effects had been minimal for her. She had lost her hair, she was constantly fatigued. She dealt with neuropathy that affected her ability to walk properly. Through all of this she was shining. She was a strong, willful, funny girl. While cancer and the treatments took their toll on her, a toll was taken on her family. We went through each day, dealing with the reality of it, often putting a positive spin on the harsh realities as a coping mechanism. We believed she would beat this. Her fight continued. Something that boggles my mind is the sheer number of other children who are fighting the same fight. So many children endure this. It makes me sad.

I enjoyed listening to Lauren's chatter. It was music to my ears after a couple of difficult weeks. Each of the drugs she was given dealt their own hand of side effects. Helping her handle achy joints and sleeplessness was tough. She was tired and fatigued, but also restless with achy knees and the need to move. We had a few sleepless nights. All things considered, she was still moved to giggles when I dribbled wine down my chin. We were hopeful for restful nights. We were thankful to be home for Thanksgiving weekend, and looking forward to spending it with some of our favourite people.

Theo

Siblings sacrifice a lot of their own childhood when another is ill, but they continue to amaze and even teach us with their patience and resilience. I often think about how Zach's life helped shape and form his brother's character. Perhaps Theo's sense of caring comes from having to be a big brother to Zach. I tried very hard to provide the love and caring Theo needed while Zach was in the hospital. I wanted to be sure to let him know that although Zachary required lots of attention and care, that would never diminish how I loved Theo for the little being that he was, and the person he would become.

After almost eighteen years, we were proud of how we'd done with our kids. They were typical siblings; they argued, bugged each other, wrestled with and annoyed one another. They also loved one another. It was shattering news for Lauren's brothers to learn of her diagnosis. They brought their own strength to our new reality, and showed us their ability to persevere.

Theo was finishing up what should have been his last year of high school. He was having trouble with English, and it looked like he wasn't going to be able to pull off a passing grade. It was hard for me to focus on this. My time was mostly spent in Hamilton at McMaster. Although I knew the importance of caring about Theo's high school marks, I was really having difficulty. He decided to take English over the summer as an online course. Good. Just the one course, online, at home. He could do this.

The summer months went by in a wave of heat, and we felt like a hot mess with trips to McMaster with Lauren. Theo was working on his course, but something wasn't right. He was a teenager, and was sleeping a lot. I was getting concerned about his health. He kept pushing through everything, still active with peers, working, but something was happening. By the end of August, the marks were in, and he had not done well with his online course. He was happy to go back to school for a victory lap. It seemed to me that the fatigue could be something more. When he got back to school, I was receiving calls from him for permission to come home and rest. He explained it away as his body not being used to the rigour of the school routine coupled with work. Mike and I encouraged and pushed him. He needed to pull himself together. How could it be that our son couldn't handle everyday life? What was happening? We wondered if perhaps he had mononucleosis. He progressively seemed unable to regulate his body temperature. At the end of September, Theo was showing signs of a stomach bug. He was vomiting a couple of times a day, and very fatigued. He was hungry but often unable to finish a plate of food. We were also noticing weight loss. Two of his classes were high physical activity. He was exhausted every day. At the beginning of October, with much persuasion, he got some blood work done following a visit to a medical clinic where he described his symptoms. Within a week, Theo's doctor called him in to discuss the results. Initially the concern seemed to be low thyroid. A few possible causes were thrown around as Theo was examined and subjected to a myriad of tests that could be done in the doctor's office. As a definitive diagnosis could not be made, the leaning was towards pericarditis or myocarditis, resulting from the flu-like symptoms he was feeling. It was possible that a virus was attacking his heart. An echo and ultrasound were to be ordered to further investigate Theo's symptoms. We were sent home with instructions to go to emergency if any chest pain was experienced.

Back in September as the new school year began, Theo took on two gym classes. He had enjoyed a summer full of work and fun activities with his friends before many of them left for university and college. With the new month and all the changes that come with the anticipation of fall, Theo decided to cut down on his fast food intake. As he went to school each day, he came home tired from the 2 hours of gym, and would often need to rest before heading to work. He started to lose weight. Prior to this, he had been complaining of not being able to sleep well. He would suffer insomnia, then sleep through the day. As a parent, part of me wanted to chalk it up to teenage normal-ness. As we neared the end of the month, he seemed to be suffering flu symptoms. He was vomiting, fatigued, and his appetite was gone. After a week, he seemed to be better, but the fatigue continued. A walk to the bathroom left him exhausted and needing to rest for an hour. I was really getting concerned, and wanted to get to the bottom of these symptoms. He just wasn't recovering. I insisted that he go to a walk-in clinic, or the doctor. He went to a clinic for an exam and was sent for blood work. By the following Friday, his results were in, and his doctor called to have him come in for review. What initially looked like a thyroid issue was eventually dismissed, and the mystery continued. With the story of the unfolding symptoms, the doctor wondered if Theo had contracted pericarditis or myocarditis. Only further tests would confirm. He wasn't sick enough at this point to be hospitalized, but any fever or acute pain would mean a trip to the ER. Over the next 2 weeks, more blood work was done, an echo, and a pending ultrasound that would end up being cancelled kept him busy. Ultimately, chest pain took Theo to emergency in Cambridge.

At this time Lauren's treatment was moving towards daily IV treatments at the clinic, which would keep us in Hamilton for two weeks. We had become accustomed to our daily lives being dictated by a treatment schedule and protocol. As we packed our things, I couldn't help but feel torn. With Theo not feeling well, I really wasn't comfortable leaving him, not knowing what was happening with his health. He reassured me that all would be fine.

Lauren

O n October 18th, Lauren was scheduled for another routine lumbar puncture with more chemo to follow. Waiting for a procedure while having to fast was always difficult. That morning we had a bit of a scare as they accessed her port, and she almost immediately felt faint, lost vision, felt nauseous and vomited.

She felt better after, as she snuggled under a warm blanket in a sick bay awaiting the call for her LP. This was the beginning of a week of chemo as we got closer to the end of this phase of her treatment.

Lauren dearly wanted her whole family to spend some time with her at Ronald McDonald House. With Theo still not feeling well, it seemed a good idea for the boys and Dad to join us. Mike brought the boys and stayed for a while. Zach and Theo stayed the night, and Lauren was thrilled. Theo was still feeling awful, with no sense of why. In a way I hoped something would happen so that I could take him to Mac emergency. They went back to Cambridge after one night, and Lauren and I looked forward to heading home after one more visit to the clinic for chemo.

The next morning, we found ourselves sitting in emergency at Mac as Lauren had awoken with a fever at 4:30 in the morning. Our plan to be home later that morning drifted away. She had no symptoms other than a headache. With some Tylenol she felt well but would be admitted for a run of antibiotics, and transfusions. This was a minor setback, but very disappointing for her. Over the next few days, her chemotherapy continued while on the ward. Her fever and headaches had resolved so we were looking forward to heading home. Unfortunately this was not to be. Following her chemo October 26th, she was discharged. As we walked to the elevator I noticed that she was struggling to scratch her ear. Her left hand was not cooperating. While she could bring her hand to her head, her fingers and hand were not functioning. This was scary to say the least. I told her we would have to turn around and walk back to the ward. She was slightly annoyed, but she knew it was the right thing to do. I could tell that she was possibly experiencing a stroke. After turning back to the ward, we saw the nurse practitioner who had discharged her. I quickly explained what was happening, as she ushered us back to the room we'd just left. As she lay down on the bed, she showed more symptoms of a stroke, and the nurse practitioner with us immediately called for the PACE (Paediatric Critical Care Response) team. While her symptoms were frightening, they were short-lived. Lauren endured many tests with no conclusive cause for the muscle weakness that she experienced. She had to be readmitted and observed. It seemed that there wouldn't be any lasting effects or damage, and for this we were grateful. The weakness did return for brief moments and then resolve. We hoped to have some answers by the next day. We were both longing to be at home. By the next day, Lauren felt as well as could be expected. She had had no other signs of the weakness that she experienced the day before. She felt tired from yesterday's chemo. We didn't have any answers as to why this happened. We hoped that the cause would be clear. We were told that this was what they would call a transient ischemic attack or TIA. The words "stroke-like event" were also used.

Hanging in the Balance

As Lauren recovered from her TIA, we hoped the tests that were done would determine a cause. Was it an enterovirus similar to the one that had two years previous infected children leaving them permanently paralyzed, or was it a thrombus caused by one of the chemotherapy drugs?

The need and desire to get back home was so great by Wednesday night, and the hope that Thursday would take us home rocked us to sleep. This hope was shattered at 4:30 in the morning. A message from Mike awoke me from a deep sleep. Theo was experiencing chest pains and they were in the ER at Cambridge Memorial. From that early hour onwards I was wracked with the indescribable feeling of needing to be in two places at once. Mike's messages came every ½ hour to update me on Theo's condition. While it was initially chest pain that brought him into the hospital, there was something else going on.

Some pain medication helped alleviate the discomfort Theo felt, and he was admitted to paediatrics for severe dehydration. The following day, the doctors at McMaster discharged Lauren, knowing that her brother was currently battling a health issue in a different hospital in a different town. After ensuring that Lauren was comfortable, we visited Theo. He seemed to be doing somewhat better. Peggy and Tad came to see him, and we filled Theo's hospital room with some laughter to hide our worry. Following an unrestful night at home, I went to see Theo and find out what a new day might bring. As his care team continued to hydrate him, other issues came up. His blood pressure started to drop, and he needed an albumin transfusion to bring up his pressures. At this point the doctor listened more to our concerns, and agreed that perhaps this was more complicated than they initially thought. The doctors felt that his condition was due to what they believed was a desire on his part to become fit; but not doing it properly. The pain he was feeling, they said, was his kidneys. My gut told me otherwise. I explained that Theo, while he had made a choice not to eat as much fast food, was happy with himself and was not trying to attain a goal for self-improvement by inflicting himself with an unhealthy diet and exercise regimen. It was then that the decision to send him to McMaster was made.

Lauren was due to head back to McMaster for an EEG to completely rule out any neurological effects from the TIA. As we left the house for the drive to Hamilton, Theo messaged me that there was a bed for him at McMaster. What a feeling it is to have one child going through cancer treatment and another on the verge of an unknown illness. I needed to be with Theo, and I also needed to be with Lauren. Inevitably, as Lauren was being wheeled off toward her EEG, Theo was being wheeled in to be admitted. They passed each other in the hallway. I spent the next hour dividing my time between Lauren's scan on the 4th floor and Theo's admission on the 3rd floor.

Following Lauren's EEG, I encouraged her doctors to discharge her. They agreed, so we went to Ronald McDonald House. I felt this would be the best way for me to ensure she was doing well, and be there for Theo while they tried to assess his health and come up with a diagnosis. Over the next few days, Theo was kept at McMaster, while the team on the ward tried to figure out his symptoms and come to a consensus. Eventually, he was seen by the endocrinologist team. It seemed that his symptoms were pointing to a disease called Addison's. In one of my googling sessions, it was one thing that had come up. The doctors explained the disease to us and, while it was daunting, I was extremely glad to have a diagnosis. The doctor explained that it was a very difficult condition to pinpoint, and years ago had probably been the cause of many deaths. Theo was fortunate to have a diagnosis, and that treatment would be life-long medication to replace the cortisone that his adrenal glands were unable to make. He would need a couple of loading doses and improvement in his overall health before they would discharge him. Lauren and I decided to go back home, and I continued to drive to McMaster each day in hopes that Theo would be able to come home. It seemed to be taking a long time, and we questioned what was happening. Theo was up each night walking the halls as his body was needing to stay active. He would often feel faint though, and he informed the nurses when this happened. By the third day following his diagnosis, he still wasn't feeling as well as he should be. The ward doctor came in with some upsetting news. The loading doses he was supposed to get were severely mismanaged. Due to this, his condition was not improving as it should. It would, but he would need to stay longer. This was a cut and dried staff error. While I was upset, I wanted to be sure that this would not happen again. The doctor and I spoke about ways to improve communication and he assured me that this sort of medication error would be investigated, discussed, and steps to eradicate medication errors of this type would be taken.

By the end of that month, we were celebrating Zach's 16th birthday. While it wasn't what we had planned, we were grateful to be together in Theo's hospital room with an awesome cake for Zach. I reflected with the kids about their medical journeys, while each of their conditions were listed as one in something, I knew that to me they were all one in a million.

Coping

When Zach was born and diagnosed, I remember wondering, why hadn't the world stopped the moment we got the diagnosis? Why was everyone still walking around, talking, laughing, working, driving, living, when our world was falling apart? Here I was again, feeling and wondering the same thing.

When a child is sick, the community feels the pain. There is tremendous adjusting and coping for extended family and friends. While the rest of the world continued on, we felt as though everything should stop. We were blessed by the love, concern and generosity of our family and friends. This helped us to go on, despite the deep-seated worry.

Emotions boil, seethe and simmer together. Watching your child lie helpless in a hospital bed brings on feelings of loss as you see your children's innocence and childhood tainted enduring medical interventions. A child should be out running, climbing, giggling with friends, not lying in a bed feeling old. There was constant worry that a germ could make them sick enough to be in critical care.

When we were given the options, palliative or transplant, Zach was just two days old. Throughout his life we have always had the threat of serious infection, bacterial or viral, taking hold of his body, immunocompromised to keep him alive.

We had always affirmed that we didn't opt for transplant for Zach to keep him sheltered from life. Of course we wanted to keep him safe, but at what cost? We would walk the fine line that is inevitable as a transplant survivor. The walk between a life lived and a life sheltered from living.

Zach has risen above each and every roadblock he has encountered. Each illness, each experience, each moment he takes and wears as a badge of courage. He lives his life learning, stumbling, falling, and rising again each day. His resilience guides him.

For me, resilience became a way to cope. I wouldn't get through without taking each moment as it came, trying to find the best of each day. This had to happen even though I knew that there would be more. More tests, more procedures, more medication, more chemo. Just more.

I often felt very drained and incapable. Why hadn't the world stopped? Why was everyone going on with their lives when ours was being torn to shreds? The mundane normal things seemed so ridiculous to me. I kept a veil of privacy as a way to cope with these raw feelings. Seeing that friends moved on. I felt left behind by life. Mourning what should have been.

We were grateful for all the support from friends and family, but we felt stuck. There were so many damn days that I was sure I was going to split in two. Other people's lives went on. Milestones were met, trips were taken. Instead we felt like we were constantly fighting for our lives. We had masks. Brave faces. Can you tell when I'm wearing mine?

Reflections

Walking with Lauren, having to be aware of her proclivity to tripping, I feel like an old granny. A walk to the corner and back hurts her knees and ankles. Side effects of dexamethasone, one of the many drugs used in the chemotherapy regime. Dex is a steroid. Steroids are horrible drugs.

Living through transplant life with Zach, and Lauren's cancer diagnosis, is like juggling while walking a tightrope; and I was given no lessons in either. You need to learn as you go, and navigate through to the best of your ability.

Having children who are immunosuppressed, you become afraid of every sneeze or cough. I often wonder how I'm not an emotional wreck, catastrophizing at every turn.

Back in 2000, when Zach was born and we were told that he would need a heart transplant, the medical team at SickKids tried to limit exposure to other families due to the nature of the wait for an organ. This was well before social media had taken hold. They didn't want families to feel they were competing with one another. As we made it to the world on the other side of waiting, I longed to connect with others who had had the same experience as us. I searched for and found some online email groups that were very helpful. I am in contact with some of them today. Some of our most cherished connections were with people we met at the RMH in Toronto. People, families, who were there due to a sick child. Plain and simple. We did not take time to compare what we were going through with our children, but rather took solace in the fact that together we were facing sobering medical complications with our children. We knew each other deep to our core.

With Lauren's diagnosis, we were thrust into this medical camaraderie again, but now our world was driven by social media. Support groups are found within social media applications. I am grateful for the connection. Glad that sharing news of the battle is made easy through this media, and saddened each and every time to learn of a new diagnosis, a recent setback, or recurrence of disease.

Theo was now part of this regrettable club. Addison's disease, which had almost killed him, was being managed with daily medication. He wouldn't survive without it, but it suppressed his immune system so that, like his brother, with medications to keep his body from rejecting his heart, and his sister, with chemotherapy to eradicate the cancer that threatened her life, he too was immune compromised.

Our Normal

Throughout a child's treatment for cancer, there are many unknowns. We were given a booklet. Not a paper, but a booklet that outlined the possible side effects of each and every drug that would have to invade her body to rid her of the cancer that threatened to take her. Most of these drugs would render her neutropenic, leaving her highly susceptible to any bacteria or virus. Many times Lauren had to be hospitalized due to neutropenic illnesses. Living through the protocol to rule out causes, when the cause might be side effects of chemo.

Being in the hospital while your friends are hanging out is emotionally distressing for a young teen. Maybe her friends were going to the mall, or a movie. Maybe they were having a slumber party. She didn't know if they were. What did it matter? She couldn't go. In the beginning everyone came. It was a wonderful show of support. But then it waned. It's understandable. We didn't even know how to fix it. Treatment is long for ALL. So fucking long. Life for all goes on. Life went on for us, for Lauren, but it was different. Did she feel alright to go out? Maybe … maybe not. She was invited to a birthday party, and I was beside myself scared that she would get sick. She went. She had a great time. Tired her out. I went too. She was a bit mad that I was there, but was secretly happy too. We were consistently amazed at Lauren's maturity during these times. Not to say it wasn't difficult … it was. Yet, she was always able to shine despite her sadness.

* * *

There were more than a few rainy days during this time, filled with worry over cancer and its harms. Most often, Lauren didn't feel like running in the rain anymore. Somehow, we did make it happen though. We stepped out onto the cool grass, making sure that we could manoeuvre safely and not fall. The joy washed over us, as did the rain, as we ran tentatively from our driveway up to the corner and back.

* * *

Being in the hospital in a room dividing you from others often with only a curtain, is no way to spend a weekend. Add a few days to that and you've got yourself an emotional and physically draining getaway. Lauren would be hooked to an IV machine for her chemo, and/or antibiotics if the tests warranted. Oftentimes, she was considered quarantined due to one or more symptoms, so would have to use a commode in the room, unable to leave her small area. The simple comforts that we all take for granted are stripped away in the name of non-contamination.

Hospitals really aren't prepared for family members needing to stay overnight. No question that every moment of any time she had to spend in the hospital, I would be there. There were times when Lauren was unwell and had to be admitted through the emergency department. This often meant hours of waiting before getting a bed in the oncology ward. The gurneys weren't quite as comfortable as the beds, but they were at least a place for children to rest when they were feeling their worst. For parents waiting with their children, the options were minimal. Most often parents were sitting in straight-backed chairs for hours, when they were the most exhausted. I recall once sleeping in a most ridiculous position, as I was completely and utterly spent. I was sitting in a chair, bent at the waist with my head on my thighs, arms and hands dangling to the floor.

When Lauren was inpatient on the ward, a single arm chair of sorts was my bed. This chair folded out to a single cot, and I was able to position it right by Lauren's bed so that if she needed me through the night I was no more than inches away.

This type of existence was slowly taking its toll on me, as tension in my shoulders and neck had me in perpetual pain. I was experiencing twitches and tics, that weren't really problematic, but they certainly were annoying. I had no doubt that these were all symptoms and signs of trauma.

Hate

Hate is a strong word. Too strong for many things. I read a news story once about a woman who had survived the holocaust. She spoke about how people of today use the word hate too frequently for things that are really mere annoyances. These words rang true for me. I encouraged my children to use the words love and hate with thoughtfulness. I make conscious decisions about when to use these words. If I don't like a particular food, or a situation that I am in, I am mindful to frame my words to say that I *dislike* it as opposed to *hating* it.

I will, however, say, "I hate cancer." There are truly few things that I would say I hate, and cancer is one of them. I hate what it has done to my daughter and to our lives. We did our best to stay positive, to be strong. I will not lie. It was hard.

I read an article that said only the person living with cancer should be the one to state what it's like. As an onlooker, a family member, a caregiver, we should not assume that what the person feels they are going through is a fight or a battle. These terms may not be true to their real feelings about their diagnosis and treatment.

I had referred to Lauren's diagnosis and treatment as just that a few times. "She has won a battle," I said when we were told she was in remission, "but the war is still on. There are many phases of treatment to go through before the war against cancer is won."

Was I using words that weren't accurate about her cancer? Was this like a war, a battle, to her? I asked her. I didn't want to use analogies and words that didn't truly describe her own thoughts and feelings. This was about her.

Lauren told me that she felt like her body was fighting against itself. That to her it was a battle.

And so we fought.

During the months and years following Zach's second transplant, we would meet other transplant families at the hospital. These families become your support. You have all been through the same hell. You have lived many of the same fears, emotions and experiences. They are family. For Zach, meeting another child who had the same scar, the same feelings, was wonderful. He was not alone. One of the fears we carry after an organ transplant is the increased risk of cancer. The immunosuppressant drugs put any recipient in danger of getting cancer. Cancer. No one wants to hear that word. Twice while at SickKids following appointments for Zach, we were visiting fellow transplant families when they were told that cancer had been found in their children. Cancer in children. Cancer in your child. Such a frightening thing to imagine. For me it was like having a brick hit me. I could only imagine what these families were feeling. After being there to hear this news for two other families, my mind tried to tell me it was an omen. It was telling me to prepare, because it was going to happen to us. I tried not to feel this way. Some would say it was thinking negatively rather than positively.

The added risks following organ transplant can be a weight. You don't want to carry that weight around. It can be cumbersome and tiring. Keeping that weight with you affects your ability to go on with life.

If cancer was ever discussed between Mike and me, it was a worry we shared when thinking about Zach's future. Never did we imagine that cancer would threaten the life of one of our other children.

It is not my intent for anyone to take this recount and compare it to someone else's. Each person's diagnosis, protocol, prognosis, reaction to drugs and treatment are very unique and personal.

I often think about our human nature to compare. By comparing, we make judgments, and put things into context, and into perspective. This mechanism is vital, I believe, to our ability to be resilient. I do feel it is important to know when it is best to use this to our own betterment, and not to the detriment of others. As a parent I believe I have a responsibility to instil a sense of self in context to the world around us. Love, family, community. I tried to encourage my children to have the ability to make important decisions and sound judgements based on caring, ethical and moral values.

We live in a shrinking world that challenges us daily to be aware of all the injustices that happen around us. Among them is the inexplicable suffering of children. We begin to die the moment we are born. Our lives unfold before us, with the expectation and hope that we will live a full and meaningful life. Somewhere in the depths of all we are and all we do, we know that each day, each minute, is one less than before. We are always moving towards that moment when our lives will cease, and what will it all have been for? We try to pack as much living into these moments, hoping that at the point that we must look back on where we've been and what we've done, we see a beautiful life behind us as death becomes the portal for what might lie ahead. We don't want to believe that a life will be cut short. Why would a child get sick? Why would a child die? What kind of injustice is that? Stolen moments of a joyful childhood replaced with hospital stays, procedures, treatment and pain.

Wrapped in this human skin, carrying this loving heart and thinking brain, I hate the injustice.

Maintenance - 2017

The final stretch. After many phases of the ALL treatment protocol, Lauren was finally starting the last but longest phase. Maintenance promised to be easier than the rest. The cocktail of chemo was mostly taken by mouth at home with monthly visits to the clinic that would include IV and intrathecal treatments. Most kids felt much better during this stage and were able to go to school. As we scratched a line through each phase as being done, we were encouraged by this promise of a closer to normal existence for all of us. Things started off fairly well, until Lauren began feeling pain in her knees. As well, her counts were dropping rather than levelling within a manageable range. Following MRIs of her legs, the joint pain was diagnosed as osteonecrosis. The steroids that were a routine part of her treatment were limiting blood flow to her bones. This was causing pain as her joints struggled to do their best under less than favourable conditions. Her bones were deteriorating and this was evident in her daily pain and dwindling desire to be mobile.

At this point, Lauren's medical team made the decision to put her steroid on hold. She was supposed to take Prednisone for 5 days every month during the one year eight-month maintenance phase. While this is an important component of this part of treatment, it was also a detriment to her well-being.

When Things Look Better

With the knowledge of what was happening to Lauren's bones, we looked for assistance from her physiotherapy consultant at McMaster. It was suggested that we get a fair assessment and referral to therapy options in Cambridge. This was early spring, and Lauren was still wearing her orthotics. She started visiting KidsAbilty's physiotherapist weekly to improve her gait and strengthen her legs. After a few weeks, working with her therapist Sharon, Lauren was feeling stronger and with effort could correct her wobbly gait. At one visit, as Sharon was measuring Lauren's ability to flex her ankles to assess her for drop, the results were surprising. It seemed that the neuropathy was significantly better. This was certainly a great relief. Using the AFOs had definitely taken some of the worry away for her safety, but the concern for her future mobility was a dark cloud hanging over us. It was quickly decided that there was no need for Lauren to wear the custom-made braces for safety. As her mobility seemed to improve, there was still pain. This was concerning, and Lauren continued to see the bone specialist at McMaster.

The Choice Between Life and Limb

We knew that steroids would take a toll on Lauren's bone health. She was at the age when bone development is at a crucial phase. Since the beginning of treatment her protocol had included short stints of Prednisone. After about nine months Lauren was complaining of pain in her knees. MRI showed deterioration in her bones, which was the cause of the pain. The plan for her treatment was quickly changed to reflect this new development. It was easy at first to be happy that Lauren could enjoy life without the side effects of steroids. Looming in the background, however, was the ever constant terror that her cancer might return. Following a seven-month break from Prednisone, we knew that re-evaluation would be necessary. Lauren was referred to an orthopaedic surgeon to further investigate her pain. Scans of her hips, knees and ankles were done. Over a number of weeks she succumbed to tests and consults as her condition was investigated. The news was less than encouraging, yet not unexpected. To continue her treatment without the use of steroids would put her at a greater risk of the leukemia returning. Continuing the protocol with steroids meant inevitable early onset arthritis at the least; joint replacements would be highly likely. Putting off the inevitable. Between a rock and a hard place. Caught between the devil and the deep blue sea. Instead of risking life and limb, we had to jeopardize one for the other.

Summer and Autumn - 2017

Lauren was still in remission. She looked good, but felt lousy. Some symptoms were concerning and pointed to relapse. Thankfully, a bone marrow aspirate procedure ruled that out. She just didn't feel well. These days were meant for fun with friends but were instead pronounced with vomiting and general fatigue.

By the end of the summer, the idea that Lauren should have another bone marrow done to check for relapse was being discussed. She was dealing with some concerning manifestations that were difficult to explain. Thankfully, it was decided that Lauren's symptoms were due to a virus. She had her regular lumbar puncture with chemotherapy without incident.

Lauren started her ninth grade in September of 2017. She was determined to do her best work, and was excited to be starting high school with her peers. Her eighth grade wasn't what she had hoped for. Most of her pared down workload was done at home. She had missed spending time with her friends, giggling in the hallways, meeting new people. Now, she wanted to make up for that and take on a full day, do all the work, spend beautiful moments like a fourteen-year-old girl should.

Through the dwindling days of 2017 Lauren did well at school. She worked hard to complete assignments and homework. When needed, she would enlist the help of me or Theo, especially for algebra. She was enjoying her Food and Nutrition course, though she often exclaimed that she wanted a greater challenge than what it offered. I was quietly proud of her motivation.

As Lauren excelled in her schoolwork, her health continued to leave us perplexed. She was in the 'easy' maintenance phase of her treatment. This was supposed to be a breeze. Instead, she was dealing with horrible mouth sores, infections on toes and fingers, haemorrhoids, and a rash on her scalp, which kept her home sick for 6 weeks. A final diagnosis was given, attributing all of these worrisome symptoms to an enterovirus similar to hand, foot and mouth disease. We continued with the prescribed treatments and known remedies to alleviate the lousy feeling that all of these sores bestowed upon Lauren.

I barely remember what Christmas was like that year. I kept my sights on July. If we could hold on until then, treatment would be complete. Lauren would have to go back to McMaster periodically for check-ups, but she'd be done, and hopefully wouldn't have any relapses. This outcome seemed attainable now. We could see the finish line ahead.

Reflections on Cancer

Before 2016 I didn't know too much about cancer treatments. When I was fourteen, my dad was diagnosed with multiple myeloma, a type of blood cancer. That diagnosis took his life following months of illness and treatment. I didn't fully understand at the time, the complexities and number of drugs and therapies used to rid a person's body of the cancer beast.

Years later when a friend was diagnosed with breast cancer, I learned more through her telling me of her experience. Not long after that my sister was diagnosed with breast cancer. Miles separated us. I could only draw on what I had been told by my friend, to understand what my sister was enduring. I had a hard time knowing what I could do. I felt strange and awkward, and I didn't call when I should have. I tried to justify my reluctance by convincing myself that she probably had a lot of people calling and she didn't need one more. Is that over-thinking? Over-rationalizing? Worrying too deeply....

I was wrong. Regardless of what I was going through, it was wrong of me not to reach out. I eventually did call and talk to her. I listened to her tell me about her diagnosis, her surgery, the treatment. I worried about her, I got updates from my mom and my sisters. She was going to be alright.

After Lauren was diagnosed, my sister called me to talk. I told her how sorry I was that I hadn't made that initial call sooner. I told her about my reluctance and how foolish I felt.

We talked more about her cancer and how she was, as well as Lauren's treatment. There were similarities, and lots of differences.

As Lauren's treatment continued, I reflected on the conversations I'd had with families, what I'd read, and what we'd learned over the past couple of years. Each person's diagnosis is very unique, which makes their treatment and journey very tailored and unique.

When someone asked me, "How is Lauren doing?" my mind immediately asked a question... "Short answer or long answer?" How I decided which to choose depended on many variables:

- Did I want to watch their face drop and eyes glaze over when I told the long version?
- Did I feel like going into detail of all the things that were happening?
- Would they understand all that was going on? When they didn't understand, would I feel like answering more questions?
- Did I want to see the pity on their face when I explained what the chemo was doing to her body?

It had been two years now since Lauren was diagnosed. Her treatment was five months from being complete. She took pills every day, that were chemotherapy. She took supplements each day to hopefully minimize the neurological side effects of one of the chemo drugs. She took medicine to alleviate the uncomfortable feeling of acid reflux due to the chemo drugs. Each week she took another chemotherapy drug by mouth. This one caused nausea, aches, fatigue, and flushing. Each month she took steroids. Steroids are a nasty drug. Once a month she went to the clinic for IV chemo. Once a month she had to inhale a medication to protect her lungs from infection. Every eight weeks she got chemo injected into her spinal cord. The regimen had been ongoing for the last fifteen months. This phase is called maintenance. It is regarded as the 'easiest' part of ALL treatment. The toll is tremendous, the price paid is huge. Lauren put on a brave face every day, facing the knowledge that although her treatment would soon be complete, the chances of relapse were there. She would be followed by oncology for the rest of her life. She would live with long-term effects from the drugs, physically and emotionally.

Turning Point - 2018

As this new year unfolded, the milestone was palpable. While Lauren was finishing up her chemo in 2018, she devised a plan. She had received confirmation from Children's Wish that she would be granted something of her choosing. She was somewhat like her sister actually. She read and reviewed, made lists, and was confident about how she wanted to spend her wish offer. She wanted to scuba dive on the Great Barrier Reef. She wanted to see Sea Turtles, stay in a resort with pools to dip in for reprieve from tropical heat. Together, Lauren and I found the perfect place. Australia. After much research Lauren agreed that Cairns would be the place to go. The paperwork was almost ready to go.

By April, Lauren would have completed two excruciating years of cancer treatment. After that, the home stretch would be around the bend. She was so close! Starting in late February, Lauren began complaining of continuously feeling unwell. She had made it through the uncomfortable enterovirus, but now something different was looming. By March, she continued with these symptoms with no relief. Her stomach was constantly in pain. By the end of March 28th during a clinic visit, an 'investigation' suggested the cause as a need for more antacid medication. The decision was made to increase the dose of her Lansoprazole. Two weeks later, on April 12th, Lauren still wasn't feeling much better. The clinic doctor felt that there were two issues at play, a worsening of acid reflux and the need for blood sugar maintenance through changes to her eating habits, specifically bedtime snacks.

I recall Lauren and I exchanging a glance at this moment. A look that said, *that's not it*. At the same time, trusting the diagnosis and plan to see if the changes would help.

Lauren's grade nine dance was on the nineteenth, and she dearly wanted to attend. I was more than a little apprehensive for her to go, given how she had been feeling. She hadn't missed any school though, and seemed to be managing as well as she could. We drove to Brantford early in the evening of April 18th with the intent to find some shoes to go with an outfit that she had for the dance. Lauren picked out a stylish pair of shoes with a bit of a heel. She was excited to be going to this dance and had already made plans with her friends. I was on alert, making sure that she had a plan in case something wasn't going well. We drove back home just as dusk was falling. As we passed by a field not too far from our home, we stopped and watched a large herd of deer as they foraged and ate in the waning light.

We arrived home, and could immediately hear that Mike was practicing on his drum kit. Lauren went inside first, leaving me to carry the remaining bags from our shopping trip into the house. As I approached the door, I could see Lauren standing at the top of the stairs, dancing to the beat of her dad's drums. She was smiling and laughing, enjoying the rhythm and the delight of being a teenager. We began to settle in, putting our purchases away. Lauren took out her new shoes and tried them on. She walked up and down the hallway, as though she were a bride preparing for her walk down the aisle.

I heard it before I saw her. Lauren had fallen and sprained her knee trying out her new shoes. She had been so glad that she no longer required her orthotics, and now she was lying on the floor in pain.

We called McMaster to get some guidance, and decided it would be best to go out to our local emergency room for an x-ray to be sure that there were no breaks. This was a real blow. Cancer once again trumping and bullying, taking over a young girl's enjoyment.

A trip to the emergency was definitely not something that we wanted to do, but there we were. We were encouraged that they were able to fast-track Lauren through due to her condition and were home fairly soon. This wasn't much comfort though, as this injury meant that Lauren wouldn't be going to the dance. She was bitterly disappointed.

By Saturday, she felt somewhat better as far as her knee was concerned, but was experiencing rectal bleeding which we attributed to haemorrhoids. By early next morning that bleeding had stopped. Overnight, Saturday to Sunday April 22, Lauren was up a lot through the night. I was sleeping beside her in case she needed any comfort and support. Early in the morning she woke me as her stomach was upset and she felt that she might vomit. I retrieved a bowl for such an event, and a cool cloth for her head. She vomited, seemed to feel a bit better, and asked for juice. She was unable to keep the juice down, and I was worrying that she would quickly become dehydrated if this pattern continued. We tried some Tylenol which came back up, and Lauren then asked me to rub her chest with Voltaren. She had never asked for this treatment before, and this was an immediate red flag to me. I called McMaster Oncology with my concerns, and it was decided that she would at the very least need IV fluids to keep her hydrated.

In retrospect, over the next hour, Lauren exhibited symptoms of the serious illness that would have her fighting for her life.

Go Gold - 2016

During one of Lauren's lumbar procedures, we met Nevan and his mom Anita. Anita and I were sitting in the recovery area of the procedure lab. The lab was not large, enough room for three recovery bays on either side of the nurses station. The one bathroom was behind the nursing station. A small room which seemed to be for staff only, a supply room, and the procedure room. Most often we would walk over from the clinic when it was Lauren's turn for her procedure. It was a well oiled machine. Each child, each procedure carefully planned and scheduled. It was a short procedure, usually lasting about ten minutes, the preparation and recovery being the longest portions.

Anita was sitting in the bay next to me, waiting for Nevan to be brought out of the procedure room to recover. Conversation between the two of us was easy and familiar. We both had children who were having lumbar punctures that day to receive chemotherapy. It was obvious that both Lauren and Nevan had leukemia. As we shared stories, we realized that we were both from Cambridge. Anita explained that we weren't the only ones. There were at least six other families who were travelling to McMaster for cancer treatments. This was Nevan's second diagnosis. Anita and her husband were adamant that the community needed to know. They wanted to raise awareness in Cambridge. People in Cambridge should know that families of this community were fighting and needed help. This was the beginning of Go Gold Cambridge.

The month of September is Childhood Cancer Awareness month, and this small grassroots group of parents and a few friends was going to make sure that Cambridge knew it! We set out on a small scale to line as many streets as we could with gold ribbons. We connected with local businesses to help with getting the word out. A flag with the gold awareness ribbon was created and flown at city hall to mark the significance. Anita and Craig's vision was to raise awareness and funds to help the families who were in the midst of a cancer fight with their child. They had high hopes and, during some of the most difficult days for their own family, were reaching out to help others.

Over the next couple of years, the incidence of childhood cancer in Cambridge would double. The families that Go Gold was supporting became a very close group. We relied on one another for emotional and familial guidance during the worst times of our lives. We were a family like no other. For many, when their child had been diagnosed, their family members distanced themselves.

For our children, it was a connection that showed them they were not alone. Right here in their own city other kids were having the same procedures. The same crappy days. Together they could laugh and cry. Many of these families remain connected; regardless of whether we see each other or not, we will always be family.

Cancer is a Thief

t steals your will if you let it. It will try to take your life. You can fight, it is strong. It is wily; it seems to know that the biggest arsenal you can bring will batter you down as much as it will weaken it.

A thief that threatens, always lurking around the corner. Hiding in the dark, dark places where you don't want your mind to go. You rally, you fight, the war rages... while the life that you knew, the friends, it all carries on as though you never left.

They think of you. They wonder, they care, but life continues. You try, you want to join in, you are only half invited. Others are not sure of what you can manage... will you be able to persevere...?

The pain. The drugs that will kill this monster may kill you. The pain. No one calls. It feels that no one cares. You have been left behind as your world goes on without you. That is pain. The tears fall silently.

No one sees. In the dark they fall and dry on your cheek. The thief. If lurks. Stealing what is most precious.

You feel powerless against its quiet rage. You instinctively want to protect. You would do anything to surrender your body to the thief. 'Take me! Steal from me, not my child!' Alas, once it has chosen its victim, its hooks are in.

Too many times cancer has stolen lives. Stolen precious lives away from families. Lives that will never be replaced. Even when we fight the thief, each battle steals something away. We rise above as often as we can, even with the loss of each part that the thief takes, we try to rise above until all the battles are in the past. The cry of a war won is heard. But the celebration is shadowed by the truth. There is always the fear that the thief will come again, as there is no guarantee that you can keep it at bay.

The thief. It allows other monsters to hide in the shadows and destroy from the inside out.

The thief. That fucking thief. With its evil comrades. It stole my daughter.

* * *

April 22, 2018

We arrived in the emergency department and it was obvious to me that Lauren was experiencing moments of confusion. The symptoms that she was displaying were worrisome. I noticed on the drive to Hamilton, that her affect was off. She was slightly lethargic, and was asking questions that were unusual for her, things she knew the answers to. She began to speak gibberish, and phrases that were almost comical but in reality very scary. I quickly relayed my concern of her cognizance to the triage nurse. She needed to get in right away. The nurse understood, and Lauren was fast-tracked through the triage process and taken to a room in the emergency department. Her care was swift and productive. The doctors and nurses quickly began treatments following a cursory but thorough look at her vitals and began to make suggestions about what we were dealing with. Was it infection in her port, overall infection? Virus? Bacteria? Quick boluses of glucose and saline were given and IV antibiotics were started. Lauren was still lethargic, with moments of lucidity that could quickly turn to confusion and odd statements. It was clear that she was experiencing shock, and the treatments were to even out her blood sugar as it was low. As her blood sugar normalized, she was still showing signs of confusion. The oncology fellow and the ICU doctor were quick to visit, and the weight on my heart began to grow heavy. I was told that Lauren's condition was serious. I heard rumblings of shock and sepsis, and felt nauseous. They said they would work to bring her out of it.

She would need treatment in the ICU. They said my quick action by bringing her in when I did had likely saved her. She was admitted to the ICU, where there was a continuous stream of doctors and nurses as they sought answers for her condition. This was a whole new team. This was not oncology. This was not cardiology, this was ICU. ICU with Lauren.

Once again I was watching one of my beloved children go through a medical trauma. The tests, the IV poles, the wires and tubes, all to hopefully, dear god hopefully, get her past this.

Sepsis and septic shock. I was familiar with this. When Zach was little, I had connected with a mother through a support email group whose son was born with the same heart defect. We never met, but we supported each other through the sisterhood of mothering a child with a heart defect. Her son would not get a transplant until 2016, when he was 6 years old. Life for him following what should have been a monumental surgery was difficult. It seemed at each turn there was illness. In February of 2017 Caleb became ill. With frequent visits to the doctor, it was not clear what was happening, except that he seemed to have influenza. The situation became dire one night as his mom rushed him to the hospital. Within hours he was declared septic and was gone. It was devastating for his mother. Since the day Caleb died, I have carried her sorrow and grief with me. So many miles separate us. We have never met, yet I know her in my bones. I would often wonder why I was feeling so much for her. Now I knew. I believe something was telling me that I too would lose my child, a year after she did. I felt profoundly sad the weeks leading up to Lauren's death but could not figure out why. I wish neither of us had to live through the devastating pain of losing a child.

* * *

Lauren was talking to me, and by late afternoon seemed to be doing better. Some of her systems and vitals were normalizing, but others were still struggling. She had multiple lines for needed medications, a foley catheter for output, and was intubated by eight o'clock that night. Before she had to be intubated, Lauren would ask many times where her dad, Theo, Zach and Sarah were. She wanted them to come and see her. After the intubation, she was awake on and off but couldn't talk to me. It didn't stop her from wanting to communicate. We did our best to use our own version of hand signals and spelling to talk. Her sense of humour still intact, she showed me her impression of her dad asleep while watching television.

Lauren needed more than one access point. The use of her port-a-cath would not be sufficient for the treatment her body needed to fight septic shock. She would also have a catheter inserted to monitor her urine output. An IV put into her right arm became interstitial, so it was necessary to move to the other arm. When I try to remember now if she had another line inserted, I can't honestly remember… the details are starting to blur from my memory; perhaps for self-preservation. My notes tell me that an arterial line and a central line at her groin were needed. A CT scan was done with contrast to see what was happening with her gut. An ultrasound looked normal.

* * *

Lauren desperately wants a drink, but they want to keep her NPO until they know what's going on.

She is now lucid and it is obvious she still has her sense of humour despite how she must be feeling. When we realize the IV is shot, I say, "Oh my look at the sausages!" She wonders aloud what I mean. "Your fingers," I say. They look like sausages from the IV not working. "Don't worry. They'll fix it."

Later she asks. "Did you save the sausages?" I have forgotten about my reference and wonder what she means... perhaps the sausages I made for breakfast the previous morning?

"The sausages, my fingers, were you able to save them?" We all laughed then!

* * *

We thought that cancer would not take the best of us. When I look back now to reflect, I wonder if I was wrong. I do feel like cancer did take the best of us. Lauren was a bright and shining light that held us together. While cancer did not take her, it is because of cancer that she is no longer with us. It angers me that it was the treatment. The incessant treatment that she was so close to finishing that took her. We feel that she was ripped from our grasp. As we move into the month of July, we grieve and mourn as though her death has just happened. We grieve and mourn what would have been a wonderful celebration of finality. The completion of the longest two years and three months of our lives.

In 2016 when we looked ahead to July 6, 2018 it was with anticipation of the end of this awful treatment for Lauren. Now as this day approaches I am filled with anger. I am so sad and angry that she didn't live to see this day. That her treatment had to end with her losing her life. It was a milestone that was to bring joy and celebration. We knew that the chances of relapse would still hang over us, but we were hopeful back then that we wouldn't let this shroud the rest of her life.

Dragonflies in April

A beautiful box was presented to us. We all sat in silence trying to comprehend, trying to make sense of what we had just been through. Inside this box there was a sheet of paper that presented a story. The story of Waterbugs and Dragonflies. Included were many simple yet elegant gold dragonfly pins.

This became a symbol for me. A children's story that was written to provide some meaningful explanation for the death of a child. The pain and anguish were like nothing I had ever experienced. A part of me was gone.

* * *

I hadn't slept much through the night. Lauren had spiked a fever. They were treating her with cryotherapy. Due to the nature of her condition they couldn't use acetaminophen or ibuprofen to bring her temperature to normal.

By mid-morning the next day, we had found an old cafeteria tray and white board marker so that Lauren could write messages. She was asking for the rest of the family. I called and left messages and sighed a bit of relief to learn they were on their way. Lauren would drift in and out of sleep, and I did my best to stay positive. Shift change on the PICU brought in a new doctor. She reviewed Lauren's case, and came in to say that she felt that the worst had passed. She was certain that she would be fine. Her body functions were trending towards normal. As I stood by her, I held her hand and talked to her. She would motion to me when she wanted to write on the board.

By early afternoon, it seemed that she was more alert, and we were given a digital means to communicate. As it was being explained, Lauren was getting increasingly agitated. It was becoming necessary to sedate her, as she had pulled on her intubation tube a couple of times. I watched as she gently fell into a medicated sleep, screaming inside that she wanted to be awake when her family arrived.

Mike, Theo and Zach walked into the intensive care unit looking slightly scared and dishevelled. Only one person was permitted to be in a patient's room at any time, but that was unacceptable given the circumstances. Lauren was still sedated. Mike and the boys prepared themselves by donning all of the necessary gloves and gowns. I stood outside the windowed room at the nurses desk watching and waiting, feeling the most unsettling mix of emotions.

Four of us sat in the family room, just steps away from the PICU where Lauren was still moored to the illness through monitors, medication lines, catheters, and sedated rest. The mood between us was distinct, but the words were those of hope and desire to move past this. I explained that Lauren was in septic shock, but that by all accounts the doctor felt that her condition was improving. Suddenly, we heard the code blue announcement. Mike shot out of his seat and ran for the doors to the ICU. We were right behind him, he called out, "It's Lauren!"

The PICU is structured so that each room has a dedicated nurse. Each room has only one patient. There is a main nurses desk in the middle of the ward, and all rooms around it are windowed, with a smaller command area for each nurse to sit while monitoring a patient. Lauren's room was full of people. Bells and alarms were filling our ears. The corridor was filled with other nurses and doctors. I was frozen. Someone positioned Theo, Zach and me into chairs in front of the window to her room. I heard Mike behind me, talking to our social worker. "This isn't how we do this. We're Destuns, we have made it through some of the most difficult moments in life. This is not happening."

* * *

We were surrounded by family and friends. People who we were distanced from due to life circumstances were coming back. Our hearts were empty. At this moment, there seemed nothing that could make me feel whole again. I kept the story of the Waterbugs and Dragonflies close to my heart. I wore the pin.

Before the service, Peggy and Allison took me out shopping for something to wear. I really didn't feel like shopping, but I was grateful for the company and knew that a change in scenery would do me some good. We made our way to a women's clothing store that was ready for a Mother's Day promotion. Right. Mother's Day was coming up. My mind had been stripped of senses worldly of time and happenings. We walked through the vestibule, and there was a sign that simply said, "Mom I'm Fine." My breath caught in my throat. I made my way to the section of pretty spring and summer blouses. There were dragonflies everywhere. I purchased a blue blouse that was printed with delicate dragonflies. Peggy and Allison found some items as well, and we made our way back home. When I opened the bag, a large postcard fell out onto the table. "Mom I'm Fine." The words were telling me that Lauren was here. She's here and she's fine.

Many family members had travelled to Cambridge to be with us. My mother and sisters Mary Jane, Linda and Heather had all arrived to be with us. Each one of them reeling as much as we were with this new reality. Throughout it all, they had been a source of support from afar. Phone calls, messages, and care packages had been sent and accepted with reciprocated love. Neighbours had offered space in their homes to host any out-of-town family. We were blessed in the face of our loss to have so many loved ones surrounding us.

The first visitation was the night before. The room filled quickly with people who knew Lauren and our family. It was dizzying. I had worn the dragonfly pin on the blue dragonfly blouse. Just minutes before the end of the visitation, I saw a lady that looked vaguely familiar come in through the doors. She made her way straight to me, calling me by name and hugged me. Seeing a face that was familiar in a different time and place was a jolt. Heather explained to me that she too had lost a daughter, fourteen years earlier at McMaster. She learned of Lauren's passing through mutual friends from high school and, now living in the same region, found it easy and felt compelled to come. We stood and talked as long as we were able. Heather put something in my hand. She said it was a duplicate of a gift that had been given to her after her daughter Kate had died. A mother daughter heart necklace. Two chains held together by the heart, to be broken and shared by mother and daughter. That chain and heart, half with Lauren, half with me, has never left my neck. Heather and I will often connect for a meal when we are able, now having a bond that is deeper than our school and home province connection.

A week later a friend of mine asked me during a visit if I was open to talking to a medium that she had a connection with a number of years ago. Shelagh explained how Mark had started talking to her one day as they both walked towards the school to each pick up their children at the end of the day. He had approached her with information, about some family information, and an issue with a seasonal building that they owned. She hadn't sought him out, and the things he told her were true. None of the things he knew could have been discovered by doing any internet search or through any conversation with a mutual friend. She had also gone to see him at public functions and told me that he was amazing. She also said that he was booking into the next year.

I decided that night to put in a request through his website for a session. The website said appointments were being booked for 2020.

The next day he emailed me that he thought he remembered me and would like to call me. The day after that, he called and we talked for an hour. He said that 2 days after Lauren died, her spirit told him that he might not remember her, but that he needed to find me, to let me know she is ok, and that I had questions that she needed to answer. He posted on his facebook page that a 14-year-old girl had connected with him and that she was sending dragonflies. On the phone he told me that we had a mutual friend, Heather. Heather told him she thought it might be my daughter. She never used my name or Lauren's. Heather came out to Lauren's visitation to see us, and later she messaged Mark and told him that she had just been to see me and that I was wearing dragonflies on my shirt.

I couldn't believe all of the things that Mark knew about Lauren and about other family members who had died. For me, this conversation provided the most peace that I had felt since Lauren had passed away. The intimate knowledge that he had could not have come from anywhere other than from those who had already gone. The messages that Lauren provided through him gave me a feeling of love, and of an ease that my soul had been needing. Her sweet caring spunky spirit had come through. It was one of the most beautiful experiences. Mark said that Lauren had a message for me. She said "Don't worry Mom, I'm fine."

I now wanted to know more. I wanted to have an understanding about this realm. Mark and I had met years before and now Lauren's death had our paths cross again. He and his husband had moved to the area and their boys went to the same school as mine. We had talked in the school yard a few times. I had sat with his boys in the library of the school the first day the family had visited.

I found Mark's ability to connect to spirit fascinating. His way of teaching about spirit and life was helpful. I was so amazed at how much speaking to a spiritual medium had helped me, that I would tell anyone, who showed an interest, about Mark.

At one point, he told me that he and I would be helping a group of parents at some point. He didn't know how it was going to happen, but it would. These parents, he said, would be grieving their children for many reasons, not just loss because of cancer. This made no sense to me at this time. I was not connected at all to a group of bereaved parents. It was only a few months since Lauren had passed. Within the year though, I was approached by a bereaved mom who wished to start a chapter of a bereavement group in the Waterloo Region. She had lost her daughter two years prior, due to a pulmonary embolism. She had become a member of a national peer support group for bereaved parents called The Compassionate Friends. At this time, there was no local chapter for this group, and she was looking for a couple of other bereaved parents to help her.

Within a few months, the Waterloo Region chapter of The Compassionate Friends had its first gathering. It was surprising, and saddening that there were more than twenty-five parents at this inaugural meeting. Three years and a worldwide pandemic later, the group still gathers monthly and has connected with more than one hundred and fifty bereaved parents.

Just months after our first meeting, Mark, as promised, provided an amazing evening with spirit for any of our members who were interested. Many parents walked away with a different perspective. Losing a child is unlike any other loss. Each parent experiencing this loss will live a grief that is completely their own. My loss and grief had led me to something that uncovered a new path for me. In doing so, paths were opened up for others as they navigated their own loss. The impact of Lauren's death had a rippling effect.

* * *

The morning was clear and sunny. I was on my way to the Portuguese Club in Cambridge that would be the starting point for a motorcycle ride for Go Gold Cambridge. I had some T-shirts to drop off to Helen. She and her husband were friends of Anita and Craig, and had been amazing supporters of Go Gold since its inception. I had never met Helen before this day, and was looking forward to talking with her in person. As I stood beside her, talking with her, she asked me about Lauren. She was aware of her, and our family's recent loss. As I talked, a dragonfly landed on my upturned hand. I had been telling Helen about Lauren, her journey, and how we missed her. The dragonfly landed and stayed. This beautiful winged insect, this symbol that I now carried with me, had made a physical connection with me. Helen and I stood, tears now streaming as I told her the significance of this moment. The dragonfly stayed with me regardless of where I went. We walked to the pavilion to talk to Helen's daughter Brianna. My emotions were getting the better of me, and I needed to find some space. I got into my car and drove.

Lauren would provide many signs to us that she was with us. Dragonflies often showed up where we least expected, and at the times we most needed. While the pain of her loss is always with us, the belief that she is showing us her presence is a healing salve.

Impact - The Ripples in the Pond

The loss was like a ripple in a pond. One stone dropped into the water creating a rippling. Once life, shorter than expected. This life, touching so many others, her death affecting so many. Like the ripples in a pond. In the midst of the overwhelming pain of loss, I realized how many people were feeling this pain too. Her brothers, cousins, aunts, uncles, friends, teachers... Lauren, in her kind, gentle and loving manner, had created a ripple in this world, and losing her was no different. Her loss was impacting so many. Suddenly we were surrounded by love and mourning all at once. People were telling us how Lauren had affected their lives in some positive way.

They say that there are stages of friends throughout one's life. That depending on where you are in your life, your group of friends may change. You may remember a group of friends from elementary school, a different group from high school, college, and work-mates. As our lives grow and evolve, so does our circle of friends. The loss of our beautiful Lauren was a pivotal point that brought our friends and family together. Reconnecting with many friends who we had lost contact with over time as our circles moved and changed. These people had come back to us. They felt the loss too. The ripples of her impact widened. It was a beautifully sad yet wonderful thing.

About a year after Lauren died, I was having dinner with a dear friend. Our children had gone to elementary school together. As usually happens, we had lost touch as our children grew, and our lives took different paths. Lauren's death had bridged a friendship from the past into the present. As we talked, she spoke of how her youngest had struggled for a few years in school, and how things were turning around. She was grateful for supports that were provided, and asked if I knew that Lauren had had a hand in helping. I was confused by this, struggling to remember how this could be. We picked through our recollections of a moment in time, and were able to piece together a truly poignant encounter. In the beginning, neither of us knew when or how it had happened, but her child had written words in a memorial to Lauren that needed clarification. How would these two paths have crossed in such a meaningful way so many years after the play and joy of young childhood had drifted into dreams? The conclusion brought us to tears as we laid the truth before us. On a particularly difficult day, my friend's son had walked out of class. Out of the school with no real goal in mind. What was on his mind was his struggle and how he wanted it to be over. Our home is about twenty minutes from the high school. It's not a direct route. Any turn made would easily take a person anywhere but to our house. On this day, he walked right by our house. At that moment, Lauren was outside our home. When they saw each other, he stopped and they chatted. She invited him in and they sat and talked. When he left, he felt a weight had been lifted. From that day forward, his struggles, though still with him, were less of a burden. He was able to move through them and past them to a new perspective.

Neither of us had known about this chance encounter until at least a year after. We had not known the importance of that day. My heart was filled with a beautiful warmth and longing as this small glimpse of Lauren was made clear to me. The person she was on that day. That moment. On a day when she was likely feeling run over from her chemo treatments, she welcomed an acquaintance into her world for a moment of comfort and helped set him on a lighter path. I would never be more proud of this person. My daughter. Her love shone through.

As I continued to search within myself to find meaning in the loss I felt, I was continually drawn to connections to Lauren through the spiritual realm. As I type these words, I know how they can be off-putting to some. The death of my daughter has changed me. It has forced me to be skeptical of things I thought I understood. I am still on a path of discovery and understanding. My grief leads me to try and make sense of the death of my child. The death of any child. As I read, and searched for answers, I continued my connection with Mark, the Olive Reader. This connection for me was very powerful for my own well-being. It was something that brought me much needed relief through my pain. I didn't broadcast my experience, but if anyone were to ask, I would tell them what had been the most helpful for me in my moments of deepest grief. I would tell them about Mark. When I reflect on this, I know that this was Lauren, spirit, helping to guide others to an important understanding of the spirit realm. These were the ripples of her life. The ripples that continue to affect a difference in people's lives.

I still struggle. Some days I am sitting in that chair watching the efforts of a medical team trying to save my daughter. Then I am pulling myself together and heading to work. Tucking it all away. Wishing for time. Waiting for life to give me a gift of clarity. Other days I am completely clear. Lauren was here for a reason. To be my daughter, a sister, a friend. But more so she was a soul with a lesson to learn. A teacher to all who would listen. When I try to make sense of this life, my moments of deep clarity (few as they may be as I am still a student) tell me that this earth is merely a small part of a vastness so amazing and huge that it is hard to comprehend. We are all part of a larger motive as our souls come together and interact with the intent to strive to this greater realization of purposeful being. I continue to try and put my loss and experience into a perspective of the greater purpose. I believe that Lauren fulfilled her purpose here. As humans, we are burdened with the pain of loss. The price of great love. For me, this is real. This is what helps me wake up every day. This is what guides me through each moment. I stumble every day. I get drawn into the humanities of our world. I try to pull myself out and place myself back on the path. Most days are hard. Each day ends with the lament that there is another in its wake. Each day begins with the sorrowful awareness that my daughter's human form is no longer with me. To say that I don't dream of my own demise would be a lie. Any bereaved parent would tell you that the desire to be with the child they have lost through death is extremely strong. This is not to say that this desire supersedes the need to be with the living. The overwhelming, all-consuming despair of loving a child you can no longer see or touch is a sorrow so deep that it can break a person into pieces. This spanning and ever stretching act of trying to hold your love for your children together within your heart is like nothing I've ever felt before. For me, this is not a cry for help. It is not an admission of desire to die by suicide. It is not a desire to die. It is a desire to mend a heart that feels broken.

To pull away from this, I try to focus and find the lesson. This may be a completely unpalatable thought for many bereaved parents. For me, it brings meaning to a broken life. If I cannot find a lesson in a moment of life, then I don't know what I'm here for. Finding the lesson in the loss of my Lauren is the beacon that centres and guides my waking moments. I may not fully comprehend at this time what the entirety of that lesson is, but I do know that it is part of a large ripple in the pond.

* * *

He noticed the half heart pendant around my neck. He was only 6 years old. Other children had asked me about it, but this time was different. "Why is it broken in half? Does your sister have it? The other piece?"

I told him, "No. The other half is with my daughter."

His big brown eyes searched mine as he asked, "...and is it sad? Is it sad that it's broken and she has the other half of your heart?"

"Yes," I said. "It is sad, sweetie."

* * *

Lying awake in the dark with your eyes open. You feel like you should see something, everything is there, but nothingness surrounds you. The jagged pain won't let you rest, although it's all your body, mind and soul want to do. You crave relief like a drug. Relief like a thirst that you cannot slake.

It was raining again. The sound of the drops hitting the window was enough to allow my tears to flow again. The rest of the family was outside talking in the driveway. Soon I heard the muffled sounds from outside and I knew. They were running barefoot in the rain.

Special Memories

Mom

Her eyes shine bright with a twinkle. Her little mouth is like the bud of a rose. We call her Lauren and we love her. As she grows, those eyes now sparkle with a bit of mischief. It is obvious that our Lauren Rose is an old soul. Our dark-haired beauty grew to live and love with a quiet intensity. But when necessary, she kicked that intensity up a notch or two. Growing up with 2 older brothers in the house, she found her voice early on. She easily sparred with them whether it was verbal or horseplay. Ours was rarely a quiet home when they were all together. She quickly earned the nickname 'MiniMom' as she scolded and bossed Theo and Zach when she felt they weren't doing what they should. It was not outside her realm to do the same thing with her dad if she believed the situation warranted it.

When she learned she had an older sister, she was elated. While time had separated them before, she embraced every moment she had with her sister and craved more. She looked up to Sarah and wanted nothing more than to spend time with her. She had a fierce love of family. During those times when we were all together, Lauren would be the first to suggest a fun board game and get all of us involved. Most of her greatest plans included the whole family. It brought her so much joy to have everyone together.

Our neighbourhood is like a family, and Lauren fit right in. I was always so proud of how she was able to relate to her peers as well as the adults in her midst. Her growing wit and sense of humour quickly garnered her as admired and loved by her neighbours.

While her last two years were difficult, she was a force of strength, and courage throughout. Her ability to continue to shine with her inner light was amazing and she warmed many hearts. She had dreams, hopes and she believed in the good in people. She amazed me by finding four leaf clovers every year on our lawn. She thought she must be so lucky, but oh my sweet girl, we were the lucky ones to have had you in our lives. It is an understatement to say that this past week has been difficult. I miss her terribly. She was my daughter, my mini-me, my best friend, my bunny. Sweet Lauren Rose, I hope you dance in the sky. Dance and soar like a dragonfly. Be peaceful and free.

Lauren was a bright and warm light in our lives. We are profoundly sad as we work through this senseless loss. I will never be the same. To hear her sweet voice call me Mama once more....

She was spunky, tenacious, loving, funny and brave. She deserved to live a full and meaningful life. We are forever changed by her being in our lives; forever changed by her sudden departure.

Lauren, sweet bunny, Mama loves you.

Lauren in Guides

Very much like many girls my age at the time, I participated in Girl Guides. I was a Brownie, and later found the group CGIT to be a wonderful connection for friends and activities. When one of Lauren's friend's moms told me that her daughter was in Sparks I was thrilled that she too could have the experiences that I so fondly remembered from my childhood.

At the beginning of the new Guiding year, Lauren had arrived at Sparks with her friend Chloe, who had been a Spark the previous year.

She was shy, but engaged. They arrived with paperwork in hand, ready to join. We were told that three other girls had been placed in the unit, and took priority over Lauren and Chloe. Amanda, the unit leader, would have to tell the girls with paper registration that the unit was full. So she did what she generally did......She let them ALL join! And she was so happy that she did.

As a Spark, Lauren participated in everything! She was the cutest Dorothy for Halloween, loved the games, and especially loved the singing. At the end of the year, she joined older girls for a day of camp where they enjoyed, and it is quite possible that we let her have her fair share of yummy s'mores, crafts, and food cooked over a fire. The day was filled with fun.

A Message from Guider Amanda Bauldry

When Lauren was a Brownie, I sent the following message to Karen & Mike: asking if they thought Lauren would like to participate in the Thinking Day event. *"Hi Karen, There is a Thinking Day event at the mall. The Brownies aren't going because it filled up too fast but the Guide unit was going, and they had one extra ticket. I am wondering if Lauren would like to come? I want to invite Lauren for a few reasons, but mainly because she is so excited and energetic when she comes to every meeting and camp, is always wearing her uniform with pride, and is ALWAYS so well behaved. I was so happy to be able to send that email. But it was Karen's response that has stayed with me through all of these years: "We were so proud to receive that invitation for Lauren to attend that very special day."*

Lauren continued on after Brownies into Guiding. She was a very proficient leader, with her patrol winning the award for best attendance. She continued to wear her uniform with pride, and set a wonderful example for the younger girls. Lauren finished her time as a Guide preparing those who would follow her, ensuring they would in turn offer a great year to the new Guides joining the unit.

I was excited that Lauren was going to continue on to be a Pathfinder. The year started at a Survivor camp run by other Pathfinders. Lauren was on the blue team. Because the girls were running the camp, Guider Amanda was able to be the Paparazzi, and she took many photos. Throughout all of the crazy tasks and challenges, Lauren never stopped smiling once. They had to name their team, and they chose "Blue Raspberries." They made a flag, built fires, got through a web, picked up marbles from ice water with their toes, tried bizarre food concoctions, and they had to unfreeze a shirt. In fact, Lauren agreed to put this barely unfrozen shirt on for the win! So there she was, in a shirt that had spent the night in the freezer, smiling from ear to ear, as was her way. Lauren took a break from Pathfinders in the beginning of her battle. I can remember the very day she returned; Amanda didn't tell the girls she was coming, as it was going to be a surprise. And it was a wonderful one. Screeches, screams, smiles, all from the girls who began to call themselves "the original six." The six of them: Lauren, Chloe, Hazel, Alison, Sarah, and Kailey. Girls who had been through the branches together, camped together, got disgustingly messy together, played flashlight games in the middle of a field in the dark at camp together. They were back together again. The group was happy. No photos were taken that day. Which is odd for Amanda. In February of 2018, they had another girl-led camp. Lauren was finally well enough to join them at camp again. It was a great weekend. The girls were still as close in Guiding as ever.

Lauren needed to be pulled in the sled through the snow, and the girls had an amazing time doing so, and getting lost in the process. It was at this camp that Lauren's sense of humour shone again, but there was something new. Lauren was quite the budding artist.

The girls remember Lauren this way, and came up with the following: Lauren is a friend to everyone, always smiling, never had a frown on her face, always positive, enthusiastic about all activities and never wanted to miss out. She was always helpful, and she liked to tell jokes. She made the people around her laugh, she loved going to camps, and all activities with girl guides. She was very smart and respectful, adventurous and was willing to try anything, and she was so strong for fighting for so long.

In Guiding a shining light, a guiding light is often referred to. A flame is not weakened by lighting a new fire, in fact, it's made stronger. As far back as Sparks. Lauren was doing good deeds for others.

In early April of 2018, Lauren made a donation of toys and books to McMaster's oncology ward using her own gift cards. Throughout her illness, Lauren had received many gift cards and saved them until this time. She told me in March what her plan was. She didn't want to purchase things for herself, but rather she wanted to shop for items that could be given to children who were going through chemotherapy treatments. As a 3rd year Pathfinder, girls generally earn their Community Service pin. Lauren posthumously received the Guiding Community Service pin as well as the 9th Year Service Star Pin.

Lauren the Friend

Lauren is remembered most by her friends as someone who was generous, smart, funny, energetic, pretty, and amazing. She was a strong and positive force in the world. She kept a smile on her face through the good and the bad. She was looked up to by her friends. Sarah's mom Shelagh and I used to say that Sarah and Lauren met before they were born as we had been pregnant with them at the same time. Sarah was 8 months older than her. I remember the day Shelagh brought Sarah to meet Lauren for the first time. Lauren was likely just days old. Before they were school-age, they were spending time together playing toddler games, giggling and dancing, playing with dolls and napping. As the girls started to babble and talk, they learned each other's names, and as the abilities dictated, the nicknames of Barah and Lolo were created. When they started school, Sarah wouldn't want to go if she found out that Lauren wasn't there. One year, Shelagh called the school to request that Lauren and Sarah be put in the same class, as Sarah loved Lauren so much. The feeling was mutual. Sarah remembers that Lauren was always there for her, had her back and was there when she needed advice.

Many photos and videos document the girl's friendship. Memories that are cherished forever.

Lauren was not only a special sister, daughter and student, but was my best friend growing up. I think when anyone thinks about Lauren or talks about her they shouldn't talk about the sickness part of her life but what Lauren was really like. She was smart, funny, energetic, pretty, and amazing. She was one of the strongest and most positive girls in the world. She kept a smile on her face through the good and the bad. I looked up to Lauren so much. Sometimes in kindergarten and elementary school I wouldn't even want to go to school if she wasn't there or going. One year my mom had to call the school and put in a request for Lauren to be in my class. This is how much love I had for her. She was always there for me, and always had my back when I needed advice. We have been together since we were born, and we had nicknames for each other that came from when we were just learning to talk. We were so little we couldn't even pronounce our own names. I would call her LoLo and she would call me Barah. I have so many memories; if I told you them all we would be here all night, but a few that stand out for me are this: Dressing up and dancing and singing in my basement, the time the goat jumped into our car at my birthday party and Lauren was the only one who wasn't scared, the grade six camping trip when we got lost and our bucket list. The main thing I just wanted to say was that Lauren had so many great qualities about her and that is why so many people loved her so much. She was smart, kind, funny, reliable, and most of all a fighter. Everyone who knew Lauren should feel so blessed. Lauren will always be in my heart forever. I am so glad I got to meet her as I know I would not have been able to get myself to high school or through life. On April 23 so many people's lives changed. So many people's hearts were broken, many tears were drawn, and many hearts are empty. But I know Lauren is safe and in peace, and will be in our hearts forever. And I have the most special angel in the world looking over me.

~ Sarah Malnerich

A Teacher's Perspective

Every year when I go to write report cards, I look up my bank of comments and use them as a skeleton when I write about my students. Every year I read over the students' comments I have saved over my 30+ years of teaching, those who don't fit the skeleton... Lauren's report is the one that always jumps out at me. She is one of a kind.

Lauren is a deep thinker. She enjoys the challenges presented and consistently strives to do her best. She has continued to demonstrate her commitment to her own learning by completing and returning her "Home Fun" activities as well as her "Snuggle Up and Read" book. Lauren does not give up easily. Her perseverance was evident when choosing and sticking with her home reading book. After some conferencing Lauren was convinced to switch from "Ramona the Brave" to "Horrible Harry and the Triple Revenge" which was a "just right" book for her. Lauren has continued to begin her assigned work promptly and as a result is successfully completing work well, and in the time allotted. She has worked hard at managing her socializing and is a more productive learner. Lauren has continued to listen attentively to lessons and to instructions. She consistently applies new learning to her independent work with minimal teacher support. Lauren has begun to push herself especially in the area of Language Arts. In her response journal about "Paddle-to-the-Sea," Lauren, on her own, wrote about a different "learning key" (from the ones that were discussed with the class) that she felt the story illustrated. She confidently backed her ideas up with substantial proof from the book. Lauren has continued to enjoy sharing her ideas and sharing her opinions during large - and small - group discussions. She has continued to graciously accept the opinions and the comments from her classmates even when they differ from her responses. Lauren almost always approaches all new learning experiences with a positive attitude, and gives each task her best effort. Lauren has continued to seek out teacher clarification when she is unsure of instructions or requires guidance with her answer. She accepts teacher and peer input willingly and strives to rework her assignments taking into consideration the "star" and "wish" comments from her classmates. This was evident when she reworked her "small moment" story to have a more interesting "hook." She has continued to ask appropriate questions to consolidate her understanding of the concepts being learned. Lauren has been working on setting personal learning goals and working towards achieving them. Congratulations, Lauren, on striving to consistently do your best! You are an amazing young learner!

Thank you for sharing your little girl with all of us at Tait Street Public School . She touched my heart.

My very deepest condolences to your entire family.

With Love, Sharon Monteiro

Bill & Pam Todd

Love and Support for her mom. For many years we have had a tradition on Mother's Day that the kids make brunch for the moms. Last year the Destuns joined us. Lauren and Zach threw themselves into the task of cooking with such enthusiasm and joy that they could be a part of something special for their mom. One of my favourite pictures, which I borrowed from Vicky, is the shared egg making between Lauren, Zach, Amy and Megan.

Later in August, Karen, Vicky, Tracy and I had our first 'concert' together. In the background was one of our biggest supporters, Lauren. She bedazzled our microphones in her favourite colour blue (also the main colour of our band) with some silver and black accents so we had some glitz on stage. She also helped her mom create one of our band costume T-shirts. I love that she did all this for her mom. I also love that she knew how much I love shiny and glittery things.

Determination. I don't know if I had really heard the term 'neuropathy' before Lauren's encounter with the condition. Lauren and Karen were walking along the sidewalk near our homes. Karen was holding Lauren's hand. Lauren's gait was off, and Karen explained how chemo sometimes had the unintended consequence of creating a challenging messaging system between the brain and the feet or hands. Lauren interjected, informing that it was temporary, and Karen shared a story of a young man who had experienced a similar side effect, but through martial arts training and perseverance had overcome the condition.

Lauren, smiling, basking in the warmth of the sun and the support of her mother, made it clear that she too would kick this thing. We never doubted it. Not for a minute. Through the smiles, laughter, and the kindness that permeated her character, there was an underlying bedrock of determination. Through every challenge there was always a clarity of intent, a quiet confidence and optimism that she would win. She believed and everyone who met her believed.

Lauren inspired. In fact, your entire family inspires. People like Lauren do not develop by accident. They occur over years, nurtured by a family whose values become deeply ingrained in each family member's character. The quiet confidence, the hope, the love, the wisdom beyond her years, the joy of life Lauren exhibited all had roots deep within her family.

We loved Lauren and how she made us rethink ourselves, silently inspiring and challenging us to be better people. Thank you, Lauren, for your many gifts and the generosity with which you shared. Mike, Karen, Theo and Zach, I cannot tell you enough or make you appreciate how lucky we are to have you as our friends and neighbours. Thank you for sharing Lauren, her life, and your lives with us.

Painted Rocks. Last year, Lauren anonymously gifted many of our gardens with painted rocks bearing the letters that spelled our family names. Accompanying the painted, lettered markers were larger painted rocks with the message, "Turn me over." When flipped, our rock read, "Ha ha ha. You're taking orders from a rock!" Other neighbours had other messages to inspire giggles and smiles.

The rocks and their messages were a conversation starter for several days as we tried to source their creator. We have several potential artists in the neighbourhood but, as it turned out, only one mastermind . . . Lauren.

When we finally connected the dots and asked if she had been the source of the new art installations, her eyes sparkled, she smiled, and laughed.

When I reflect on my memories of Lauren, more often than not, I find myself reflecting on the lasting impressions more than specific events. In summer, Lauren and Zach were frequent, welcome visitors at our pool. They were inseparable. Amidst the cannonball contests and swimming races, their laughter reigned supreme. And that is the point of this memory. Lauren's and Zach's laughter.

Through the summers, regardless of the various curve balls both were thrown, they challenged each other, they supported each other, and they laughed. I don't recall either crying - ever. Last summer, I remember Lauren being whitewashed with sunscreen, joking with Karen, clearly excited to swim. When I was a kid dealing with persistent ear infections, I stopped swimming because I was too self-conscious about the bathing cap the doctor insisted I wear. Not Lauren. She was confidence and enthusiasm in a delightful blend. I confess to being a bit anxious as she prepared to jump into the pool, fearing how she might fare in the water. No need. She was Lauren — leaping, laughing, splashing, playing with Zach and anyone else who dared enter the water. I loved her laughter. I loved how, in the face of challenges that would make the bravest cry, Lauren could laugh, Lauren could live, and Lauren could be herself.

Gabby

While preparing this speech, I was at a loss for words. I didn't know how to fit the past ten amazing years of my life into a one-minute paragraph. On Monday April 23rd, my life changed forever. All of ours did. All who knew Lauren were blessed to have been a part of her life. Lauren was more than an amazing student, daughter, sister, and friend. She was an amazing person, beautiful inside and out. Lauren was the light in a world full of darkness. I think I speak on behalf of everyone when I say I am thankful to have crossed paths with her, or like in the book Paper Towns, I am glad our strings crossed. Lauren would know what I'm talking about. It is hard to let go, to say goodbye. I still haven't wrapped my head around the fact that I will not see her around at school or be able to call her to hang out. But I know that she is here with me, in spirit and in my memories, which are the strongest things of all.

There are a million different things that I love about Lauren. Like the way she could make me happy just by smiling at me. She would listen to me whenever I had a bad day. She was there for me no matter what. It is very hard to lose someone like Lauren, who loved unconditionally. She made me strong just by being strong herself. I do not want to say goodbye to Lauren, even though I know that it is not forever. Lauren made me who I am today and I will continue to live out her legacy. I am blessed to call her my best friend.

In grade 7, Lauren and I were in a girls' empowerment group and she shared a quote with me. She believed in these words, and lived by them. Please join me in carrying Lauren's message throughout your own life:

I am strong, because I know my weaknesses
I am beautiful, because I am aware of my flaws
I am fearless, because I learned to recognize illusion
from reality
I am wise, because I learn from my mistakes
I can love, because I have felt hate
And I can laugh because I have known sadness.

~Rebecca Ann Totten

Amy Todd

I remember a summer when I was home during school. My dad mentioned that Zach and Lauren might be coming by later in the day for a swim. I had had the pleasure of meeting Zach on a few occasions by that point, usually making fun of me (in good nature of course!). But I had yet to meet Lauren except in passing.

I met them at the door later that afternoon. Zach did most of the talking upon the initial greet. Despite her silence, it seemed to me that Lauren was brimming with energy, almost vibrating with anticipation for a fun afternoon. But she waited patiently until the pleasantries were over.

Confirming my suspicions, she practically raced to our backyard door and was in the pool before I think the water even registered a splash. Inside I could hear her challenging her brother to a cannonball contest. I was asked to judge and - if my memory is correct - she won. By a lot. I do not know how one so willowy could evacuate so much water from that pool.

Her banter with her family during other neighbourhood gatherings was always hilarious too. I remember comparing myself at one point after a great repartee with her dad: "Was I that funny when I was her age? Am I that funny now? Damn!"

I will always remember these good times. The memories of her wit and laughter will always stick. But they will pale in comparison to the memory of Lauren, not in a single instant or a specific memory, but the feeling of quiet, gentle kindness that I feel when I think of her. I cannot tell you why I have this feeling, what specific event makes me remember her as such.

My guess is this, though: the people who stick with us, who fill us with a desire to be more, are the people imbued with a sense of self, an unabashed will to be who they are. The feeling that fills my mind and heart when I think of her makes me want to be a kinder, gentler woman. To say nothing of her bravery and strength.

I know these anecdotes and thoughts will not ease your pain. I thought it important to know that Lauren taught a woman a decade older than her how to be better. I'm sure I'm not the only one.

I love you all, and have been thinking of you all week. As with the rest of the neighbourhood, I will be here for you always. I will be there this weekend to celebrate Lauren's life, and look forward to seeing you all.

From Lauren's Memorial Book 2018

Lauren Rose Destun had a true talent for helping others reach their full potential, and brought out the best in those who sought her help. Lauren was a forward-looking young woman whose personality was filled with empathy toward everyone she met. She could be quiet and reserved, but her style of communication was authentic and direct. An excellent communicator, Lauren was a master at using imagery when she explained her ideas and concepts. She seemed to have an endless supply of innovative concepts and strategies for how to help those around her. Her sensitivity, kindness and generous attitude made her a wonderful friend for all who knew her.

From the time she was born, Lauren showed a deep concern for others. She was a giving and caring individual, ethical, and full of integrity and warmth. Lauren came into this world on August 27, 2003 at Cambridge Memorial Hospital to parents Mike and Karen Destun.

Because fellowship was so important to her, Lauren promoted harmony with her family. She was raised with three siblings; she had an older sister, Sarah, and two older brothers, Theo and Zach. Lauren was the family diplomat. She helped to settle problems and conflicts, and kept the family running smoothly. She also possessed the ability to stir things up when she needed some amusement. She loved to laugh with her brothers, and would often engage in practical jokes and rough-housing. Lauren enjoyed connecting with her family through her favourite pastimes. She loved playing solitaire alongside her mom, enjoying the Toronto Maple Leafs and Blue Jays with her dad, teasing Zach on Facebook, predicting what was going to happen on The Flash with Theo, and being inspired in her artwork by Sarah.

As a young girl, Lauren interacted well with other children. She was helpful and caring in her relationships. She was an independent person who had a vivid imagination. Lauren had a number of interests in her youth. She was a dynamic child who loved spending time with family and friends, regardless of the activity. She was an avid member of Girl Guides of Canada, starting with Sparks, to Brownies, to Girl Guides and Pathfinders.

In her spare time she liked to watch cooking shows, drama and comedy shows like Friends, The Big Bang Theory, Murdoch Mysteries, This is Us, and The Amazing Race. The Flash was her favourite television show. The cooking shows were inspiration for her to get in the kitchen and cook for herself and the family. She was becoming quite the accomplished creator, experimenting with her favourite foods and dishes. She also enjoyed art and loved to draw, paint, and participate in various crafts. Lauren loved music, singing and dancing. She enjoyed singing in the Tait Street school choir during her years there, and was also part of the Kodaly Choir. She had a wide taste in music, enjoying top 40 music as well as hits from her parents' generation. When she was younger, she often danced and sang impromptu creations, especially if there was a video camera rolling. Her favourite music artists were Ed Sheeran and Walk off the Earth. Over the last few years, Lauren would spend time watching her favourite YouTube Vloggers, Roman Atwood and Dude Perfect. When she watched their videos it cleared her mind and cheered her up. Lauren also enjoyed watching carpool Karaoke with her family. The music and comedy appealed to the whole family, and Lauren enjoyed this type of togetherness.

Some of Lauren's memorable achievements included the Victoria D'Agostino Book Award in 2015 at Tait Street Public School, Caber Toss Champion at St. Andrews Public School in 2015, chess awards in elementary school, as well as volunteering for the Beer Store Leukemia Bottle Drive in 2015 and 2017.

Lauren was one who put forth her best effort in every aspect of her life, and that carried over to her participation in sports as well. Her sense of diligence inspired others and in turn drew best efforts from her teammates. In elementary school, Lauren played soccer, road hockey, track and field, and volleyball. Lauren was also something of a sports fan, and enjoyed following her favourite events whenever she got the opportunity. Tops on her list were the Toronto Maple Leafs and the Toronto Blue Jays.

A good student who was enthusiastic about learning, Lauren was considered by many to be a high achiever. She enjoyed some classes more than others, having favourite courses and teachers. While Lauren did not get to graduate from high school, she set a big goal for herself of achieving honours. For a number of weeks nearing the end of her first semester in grade nine, Lauren was too ill to go to school, but worked diligently at home to ensure that she completed assignments and homework, and prepared for the semester's final exams. Due to her dedication and work ethic, Lauren accomplished her goal of honours for her first semester of grade nine.

Able to maintain a positive focus on the potential good to be found in others, Lauren was always ready with solid advice and guidance to offer her group of friends. She was generally friendly to all who knew her, yet to some she seemed quite independent. For those who really knew Lauren, they recognized that she could be full of surprises. Lauren enjoyed a small but solid group of true friends. She would willingly support those friends when they needed it. Because of her ability to read people, she had an uncanny knack for knowing when a friend needed help. Lauren's friends were each special to her for their uniqueness. She valued each for who they were and what they did together. One friend was her 'dream friend,' as they would spend time talking about their future dreams and aspirations. Other friends were her 'artsy' friends as they engaged in the joy of being creative together. While growing up, some of her best friends were Sarah Malnerich, Gabby Vlach, Meaghan Law, Chloe Peach, Callie Mundy, and Hazel Bauldry. After her diagnosis of leukemia, she treasured her connections with Roxy Madison, Sophie Visca, Danielle Comini, Sheldon Vitorino, Karter Ellis, Nevan Langlois, Jaxon McKinney, Olivia Hazen, and Makena Noble. She felt the loss of two girls who she met at McMaster Hospital, Claire Sommer and Chelsea Visentin.

Lauren possessed strong skills in long-range planning and project completion, a quality that came in handy when helping with her family's travel and vacation planning. Some of her favourite vacations included camping trips, Cyprus Lake, Turkey Point, and Disney for her brother's Wish Trip. Just prior to her passing, Lauren was in the midst of dreaming about and planning her Wish Trip. She was meticulous about finding the perfect destination that would help fulfil her plan to enjoy many outdoor and water activities like zip lining, cave diving and swimming with dolphins.

Lauren was a lover of animals and cherished her pets. She loved dogs and cats, especially her own dog Kelso, the family pet. They were best friends for four years.

Lauren was an affectionate soul and was sure to get a hug from family members at least once a day. She believed that hugs and smiles would help anyone through a difficult time. She had an impish sense of humour and loved to laugh. Precious moments were spent being silly and giggling to the point of sore cheeks and bellyaches of the best kind.

Lauren passed away on April 23, 2018 at McMaster Children's Hospital. Lauren was three months from finishing her treatment for leukemia. In the end, an overwhelming infection that her body couldn't withstand took her life.

Though she could be a private person at times, Lauren was always able and willing to give of herself. She was so in tune with others that she often seemed able to read their minds. Lauren carried with her an almost mystical sense of life. She was a person who was highly original in her thinking and used metaphors and symbols to describe many aspects of her life. A poetic, intuitive "teacher," Lauren Rose Destun shared herself freely, and family and friends will remember Lauren for the strength of her convictions, and love for family, life, and living with joy.

Vicky Cole

Lauren and I will always share a special memory of her birthday two years ago, when we were deciding what she wanted for her birthday present. The humble young lady would not give me an answer as far as what she would like for her birthday. I told her that if she didn't give me an idea, I would give her the ugliest socks that I could find. She still continued to tell me that she didn't want anything. The day of the birthday party came, and I told Lauren that she would be very surprised about her gift. She opened the present and found the ugliest pair of green socks with caterpillars on them. She, in true comedic form, put the socks on and proudly wore them at her birthday party. I will never forget that day. She was the sweetest girl you could possibly know, with not an ounce of greed in her body. I will cherish the lovely stones that I found in my garden that Lauren made not only for me but also for many of our neighbours. We display these stones in loving memory of this wonderful young lady. Rest in peace, sweet Lauren. We will love you forever.

Ginny Carnevale

My clearest memory of Lauren is from when she was in Girl Guides with my daughter, Sarah. The Guides were putting on a Cabaret show for friends and family at their last meeting of the year, and the girls were all contributing to the show. And in her turn, I remember seeing smiley little Lauren with a couple of her Guide friends stand up in front of a big room full of people and sing "Brave" by Sara Bareilles. I remember being amazed, and a bit envious, of her quiet confidence and her nerve to get up in front of all those people. I remember thinking, "That's a big voice from such a small person!" I really didn't know Lauren very well, but from what I did know and see, it was clear that she was a kind, compassionate, caring human being who deserved more than this. The world will be a lesser place without her in it. I am heartbroken for the Destun family, and send all of my love and strength to you all.

Shelagh Malnerich

I have so many memories of Lauren over the years, but the one that sticks out in my mind was Lauren at Sarah's 5th birthday party. John and I took 5 or 6 kids to a farm where they could ride a horse and have a sleigh ride. After the party was finished, we loaded the girls up into our minivan – all were in car seats or boosters at that time. We had both side doors open in our van in order to ensure they were safely buckled. While assisting the final girl into her seat, a large goat jumped into the front seat of the van and started to eat all the waivers along with tissue from a gift bag. As we attempted to get this big horned goat out of the van, he attempted to visit the girls in the back seat! A few of the girls were crying with fear, but not sweet little Lauren! She was right in the middle of the action, laughing and giggling up a storm, petting the side of the goat as brave as can be! Lauren's sense of confidence, fun loving spirit and adventure will never be forgotten, and she will hold a special place in our hearts forever. Sending much love to Mike, Karen, Theo and Zach. Please know we share in your grief.

Karen Pike

My most vivid memories of Lauren are from about ages 3 to 8 when her family would come to visit the farm. Along with her brothers and my children, they would spend time taking turns on the snowmobile, playing at the barn, or jumping on the trampoline. From the kitchen, I'd be waiting to hear the pack of returning kids, and one of the first things I would hear was Lauren's laughter. What a great laugh! She knew how to seize the day.

Isabella Polesky

I'll never forget the day when all of the cousins were playing at the park, loads of laughs included. There were only 2 swings, so all the girls were taking turns swinging and pushing each other. I had just hopped off and was playing around in the grass, and Lauren happily jumped off the swing and told me it could be my turn again. This truly represented her, always giving and wanting to make sure that everyone was happy.

Family get-togethers will never be the same without her big smile, welcoming words, and hilarious sense of humour. Love forever.

Peggy Dreyer

We have many wonderful memories of Lauren, and will cherish them always. One that stands out though is "Stanley pants." The Destun family had spent the night at our place. In the morning, Lauren decided to try our cat, Stanley's crinkle toy pants on, and they fit!! She strutted around the kitchen, stopping in front of us to shake her "booty." The more we laughed, the more she strutted.

Rest easy beautiful girl, we love and miss you so much.

Brenda Ross

Lauren attended the Nolan Melchin Memorial Golf tournament in 2017. I was injured and was unable to golf that year, so I was volunteering at the course. I asked Mike and Karen if it would be ok if Lauren could drive the golf cart when we would go out on the course to sell raffle tickets. They said that was fine. I asked Lauren if she had ever driven a golf cart and she said no. I asked her if she wanted to and she was all in. It was a bit of a wild ride at first but she was having a blast. She was so excited when we got to the hole where her dad and brothers were playing. Her eyes lit up and I could tell how excited they were for her. We talked about her grad dress, the colour, her shoes, and how she needed to practice walking in them. Also her love for cooking. I asked her several times if she was tired or wanted to go back to the clubhouse, or if she wanted to keep driving. Every time the answer was the same. "Keep driving." When it was time to go back, Lauren went straight to work. She hung all the stained-glass ornaments on the windows. Helped with the auction items. She was there to work. To contribute. To make a difference. And have fun doing it. I could see in the brief time I spent with her that this is how she lived her life. That was a special day I will treasure forever. It was an honour to get a day with Lauren.

Mary Mooney

My memories of Lauren are from when she was a baby, toddler, and little girl. While living in Toronto, we would sometimes visit the Destuns in Cambridge. More often we would see them in Toronto on their trips to SickKids for Zach's appointments. Often it was only Karen and Zach, but sometimes Lauren and/or Theo would come too. On one visit, Zach was admitted to the hospital and I offered to take Lauren home with me for the night. She was a toddler and it would have been a long night in the hospital room. I carried her in Karen's sling, and we took the subway to our apartment on Montclair Ave. She had a great time chasing our cat, Max, around the apartment! Dre and I had so much fun looking after her. When it was time for bed she started to get upset; missing home and her family. I held her and rocked her until she fell asleep. The next morning, I had to go into work before I could take the day off to spend at the hospital. Lauren and I travelled by subway and streetcar to downtown Toronto at rush hour, with her snuggled close in the sling. She stomped around my office in her tiny winter boots - feisty and fearless; smiling and "talking" to my co-workers. I so clearly remember the reunion with her mom at SickKids. Joyful smiles, open arms! I have many memories of this sweet girl, but this one stands out. It felt so special and exciting for me and Dre to have this one-on-one overnight adventure with her. I remember when she was born. I remember her at our wedding with her curls and red dress. I remember Lauren, Zach and Theo playing with my kids and loving their time together. I remember when I had my first girl and she suggested the name Tia. I remember visiting the new house and her showing me her room - I was so impressed with her self-portrait paintings on the walls. Although it's been many years since we've seen Lauren, she and her family have remained with us in our thoughts and hearts as she battled cancer. Lauren will be forever loved, missed, and remembered by her Mooney/Mellema cousins.

Valerie Polesky

My earliest memory of Lauren is from a Thanksgiving get-together at our old house, one of the earliest 'Poleskyloozas.' I have laughed at this memory with Karen many times since that day. There was no shortage of little girls in our families (thank you Alli) and while playing after dinner that night, they had come across a bowl of fake pears I kept as decoration in the family room. One of the cheekier girls (probably mine) had thought it was funny to stuff their shirts with the fake pears and pretend they were ladies, prancing around the room and giggling hysterically. Lauren, hesitant at first, joined in the fun and they danced around laughing and carrying on for quite some time. Lauren, not one to initiate 'naughtiness' or push boundaries, but definitely one to recognize an opportunity to have a good time and live it up with her cousins.

The other vivid memory I have of Lauren is from an Easter we celebrated at Sterling McGregor, when the kids hunted for eggs in the backyard. Chaos ensued with a dozen kids running around, and Lauren leading her baby cousin Jordynn by the hand, helping her find eggs but also making sure she didn't get run over in the process. Such a gentle, caring soul with a little cheek peppered in for good measure.

We will miss Lauren dearly; 'Poleskyloozas' will never be the same without her amazing smile.

Ellen Bartlett

I remember the first time our children met was in 2015. Lauren and Zach were home, and invited Erica and Derek to the park and then to hang at the house. Lauren treated them like they knew each other for a long time. She reminded me of Karen at that age; such a kind, gentle spirit with a magnetic personality. Karen and I chatted until it was dark but tried to get pictures outside. I remember how hard Lauren laughed when I tried figuring that out!

Lauren most certainly did not live enough years, but it certainly feels she filled every day she had with laughter, love and kindness.

Feeling blessed to have known Lauren! My heart goes out to Karen, Mike, Sarah, Theo and Zach.

Love Ellen and my family, Marty, Erica and Derek Bartlett, Truro, NS

Chantal Menchenton

I remember when I was new to Tait Street as a staff member, and Lauren and her friends would often have lunch with me. This became a regular occurrence all through her grade 5 and grade 6 years. She helped me with my recess groups with younger students, and she would often take the lead and ask to plan the games. I appreciate how much the students loved her games, and how she made them laugh. And when the students started to call me Mrs. Marshmallow, she would join right along with that huge smile of hers! I also remember how excited Lauren was about the lunch we ate at the "Safe, Caring and Inclusive Schools" workshop that we attended with Karen and other school staff. She was an amazing young lady with a vibrant personality! Rest freely Lauren, you will be missed.

Heather Lauther

My niece Lauren has touched my heart forever, and has made me to be more thankful for the small things in life that really matter. We only met in person when she was a baby, her first trip to Nova Scotia for her cousin Mary's wedding. Distance has kept our families apart from seeing each other in person over the years, but our love for each other doesn't change. I was saddened to hear about Lauren's diagnosis, and tried to be as supportive and loving to her as possible, and to let her know her family in NS was behind her and loved her very much. Her journey wasn't supposed to come to an end in this way; I prayed for her to get better and thought of her every single day. Lauren was one special girl, always had a smile on her face and thinking of others during her own battle. Love you Lauren, forever & always in our hearts. You'll be watching over us from heaven with your grandpa, nanny, great aunt & uncle, and great grandparents.

Karen Priestman

My good friend Karen was pregnant again! A girl this time. What will her name be? We went through the names we liked. Lauren Rose...beautiful...just like that little girl turned out to be. My memories of early days are like the kids in this perfect Christmas picture. Children of light and love and laughter, begat from two people of light and love and laughter. But real people, honest people. When we moved away, we lost that close contact, but the Destun family became the only link we cared to keep in touch with whenever we came to town. The memories and laughs were the same no matter what time had passed. And when the awful news came about Lauren's cancer, it felt personal. No. Not this girl. Not this family. Nobody deserves such a diagnosis, but this family is the least of any I know or have any known. But the grace and determination the whole family showed in the face of adversity time and again, and Lauren the epitome of that grace...it leaves me humbled even now.

I bought Lauren a Dammit Doll because, as much grace, light, laughter and love that everyone met the cancer with, I thought maybe she might like to just be angry. A lot. And have something to take it out on. I should have bought one for myself too. I need it now.

To Karen, Mike, Theo and Zack, my heart breaks for you and with you. You guys have been through too much already to have to deal with this devastation. But know that Lauren was loved, and shed light to so many. You are not the only ones who were blessed to have known her. Remember Karen, on one of our walks, we talked about/had read about positive emotional energy actually being a physically measurable reality? Well, I truly believe that the universal balance of good has not altered - Lauren's positive energy is still reverberating in the hearts, souls, and very earth that she inhabited in person. All my love. Karen xoxo

Julie White

Such a beautiful, wise, old soul. Long summer days with road trips in the van, at the beach, playing in the yard and years of daily walks back and forth to Tait Street School. So hard to pick a favourite memory as Lauren and the boys are so much a part of so many happy memories with my own kids. One of my favourite days was when all of the boys were at school and I was watching Lauren and Chloe. We were making chocolate chip cookies in my kitchen. There was flour and sugar and dough everywhere, and the house was filled with the chatter and giggles of little girls, which was definitely a rarity in a house full of boys. I never bake without thinking of that day, the giggles and those smiles. Karen, Mike, Theo, Zach and Lauren, thank you for all of the love, light and laughter you have brought to our lives. We will remember and cherish those sweet summer days of childhood.

Simon Priestman

Lauren and her family attended our wedding 21st July 2017, friends of my now wife for many years! I had heard of Lauren's fight with cancer, and was excited to meet this gutsy little lady! She came and danced, laughed and smiled like any other teenager with her brothers Theo and Zach and her mum and dad! A true fighter with so much love from her family and lots of support.

She came to both me and Karen and gave us a big hug at the end of the night and thanked us!

We both watched her progress and thought she was doing great with a number of very humorous text messages back and forth on our return to the UK.

It has saddened us both to hear the tragic news, but one thing I will always remember is that beautiful smile and the hugs we received.

I find it hard to express with words our deep sorrow for the rest of the family left behind to cope without a special family member.

Fly high little lady, and see you again someday.

Jake White

I remember one year at a New Year's Eve party, I had fallen asleep on the couch. I woke up sometime later to Lauren giggling uncontrollably. It wasn't until later that night when I got home that I realized she had painted my toenails a bright sparkling pink! Lauren was so full of positive energy, it was impossible not to be in a good mood when she was around. She had this profoundly funny sense of humour, and would say the last thing you would expect to come out of the mouth of a sweet little girl. Lauren had the ability to make you see past the fog and into the light, no matter the circumstances. She was truly loved by all, and the positive influences she had will forever stay with me, and everyone her heart touched.

Part 2

When She Was Dying

The Room - 2023

The sun was too bright, especially after the grey and dismal days that had drawn out the last few weeks, as though in a shroud. She lay curled up under a crumpled sheet, not facing the window. One person alone didn't need this much room. It was like an empty apartment, with a bed conspicuously jutting out from one wall. Anything she needed was crowded around the bed. A bedside table holding a few random items was just within reach. The call button, bed controls and TV controls were here for easy access. The tray table to hold her meals was beside it. It would take some effort to reach. Her cell phone lay on the towel that was draped over the table. She chose to face the wall. What lay behind her were reminders of a world that seemed a lifetime away. A built-in wardrobe with drawers and a shelf that was littered with items that for her were barely meaningful. The flowers still held their beauty to the eyes of anyone but her. To her they just stung with the pain of her reality. Abandoned food containers, brought in with the hopes of consumption, to be thwarted by nausea. A walker and a lounge chair sat empty, except for the large plastic lined basin that could be necessary when her stomach refused to keep any food down. Two couches randomly set, looking out of place, as the room was still quite empty despite the unused furniture. Nights and days blended into one another with little courtesy to allow her to know the difference. The low airy sound of the large fan at the foot of her bed helped to break the dead silence that filled the room.

She asked for the blind to be pulled down to block out the rays of vitamin D that threatened her denial. She really only wanted to sleep. It seemed to her, a constant parade of people wanting the best for her.

Looking In

How do you describe life after death? Anything that comes to mind seems like a cliche. Losing a child. A pain like no other. The loss is immeasurable. Yet the expectation to go on is unmistakable. After losing our Lauren, the years that followed were empty, yet interspersed with love and support. Grief doesn't shrink or go away, yet instead you grow around your grief. It becomes a facet of your life, your being, your every breath.

So now, the absolute shock that was felt when Sarah broke the news that she had breast cancer was enough to paralyze me. The lump had been discovered at the end of the summer. The pandemic was almost a year old at that point, and the medical system was on life support. Tests, appointments, surgeries were all back-logged. By the time the results were in, it was Christmas.

Our life had been a tale of tragedy, peppered with love and resilience. Surely we had endured enough pain when Lauren had died. God knows we had been in enough hospital rooms over the past twenty years. We couldn't fathom that cancer would yet again threaten to take one of our daughters. I had to be a strong and knowledgeable medical mother, advocating for the best care of all three of our children. Each time I was brought to my knees. It was unthinkable that my stepdaughter Sarah, the daughter of my husband, could be facing cancer treatments.

Heal Thyself

Sarah's sister had died. She felt sure that it was the chemotherapy. It's a poison. It kills the cancer but it kills the sufferers too. She wanted nothing to do with the western medicine approaches to disease. She was choosing to take this full on, her own way. She had always done things her own way. She was cautious and particular. She took her time with everything. She believed in alternative healthcare. She had a sense for the power of positive thinking, the spirit world and crystals. Natural was the way to go. To deny the disease was to heal it. She would not give it power.

Throughout her life she sought the sense of control that she longed for. She had made a promise to herself that she would do life her way. She appreciated the knowledge of natural remedies, and hoped she could rely on that. Everyone around her wanted to know what was happening. It was very difficult to talk about what she was experiencing.

When Sarah had discovered the lump in August of 2020, she didn't want to believe it. She was thirty-two. Her life was just beginning to go the way she wanted it to. Her job gave her opportunities to do the reading that she felt was opening her up to her true self. The house that she and her fiancé had bought together was a perfect little starter home. They tended to it together and planned to continue their lives here as a married couple. The ring had been bought, and they made a promise together in the garden amongst the flowers that she had so painstakingly picked to reflect the palette she wanted. The dreams she had seemed to be out of reach now. The mass. This lump. It was getting bigger.

It took five months for them to get her in for a biopsy. She just couldn't process it at all. The result showed triple negative breast cancer, the most difficult to treat. She decided that she wasn't going to do chemotherapy. She couldn't. It had killed her sister.

Living With Loss

Losing her sister Lauren had been devastating for Sarah. When they met, Lauren was young, only 4 years old. She was able to be a big sister. Something she had always wanted. Realizing that she was now a sibling to three kids made her heart skip. Relationships with her brothers and sister were forming and growing as they spent time together. Just before Lauren got sick, the two of them were beginning to enjoy things together as sisters. It wasn't fair that another sister had been ripped away from her. She had lost another sister so long ago, and the loss of Lauren brought back the pain she had felt when her sister Lyla had died. The two losses were so very different, and yet, the sheer impact of the sharp and quick way with which they both left her was similar. When Sarah was eight, she and her mother had built a family with Lyle. He meant the world to Sarah as her stepfather, and she was excited to welcome their new baby as her sibling. She wanted to be a big sister, and knowing that Lyla was coming made her feel like one. It was heart-breaking for all of them. Something had happened to this beautiful life within Audrey's womb. They were never able to come to any answers as to why or what had happened. Sarah's little sister Lyla had been born still. Her mother had to go through all of the labour, as though her sweet little baby were going to be born into their lives to hold and love, grow and live. Instead, she gave birth to her and had to say goodbye. It was devastating, and so hard to understand. It was a tremendous and traumatic loss for all of them. The loss of a child, regardless of their age or the way in which they died, is one that changes you forever. Sibling loss at a young age doesn't make sense. Out of order death. So unfair.

Sarah often asked her mother about her sister Lyla's funeral. She wanted to know why she hadn't gone. It had been a difficult decision at the time for Audrey. How do you protect a child from the misery, the pain of losing a sibling at such a young age? It was something that Audrey and Sarah often spoke about.

The loss of both of her sisters—one she had only known as a growing being in her mother's womb, the other as a person she was just starting to really connect to—had changed her.

The Love We Share

Having Sarah as my stepdaughter was a blessing. From the time our relationship had begun, I had known about Sarah, Mike's daughter. Sarah had been a part of our family since she was nineteen, and I loved her as my own. It was never an intention to step in as her mother. Sarah's mother Audrey and family were hers, and I would never overstep those relationships.

By the time she was eighteen, Sarah already knew that she could ask and learn about who her father was. She had grown up knowing only her mother's side of the family. Her life had been full and loving. She had always known that she could learn about her father when she was ready. When she decided to find out who he was and how to find him, Sarah was nineteen. She turned to facebook and reached out to me. She wanted to learn about her dad before meeting him. Sarah had taken a year to sort through these next steps. At the age of twenty, she was meeting her dad for the first time.

Mike was nervous. His life without knowing his daughter Sarah was filled with regret. He wasn't proud of how he had let it all play out twenty years ago. His mother had played a big role in that. He had always held her in his heart, and held the regret there too, but how would he now make that all up to Sarah?

He wanted to do anything he could to bring Sarah in as a part of the family we had built. We were a happy family with our three children, open to welcoming Sarah, their sister.

* * *

Camping was always a lot of fun. The trailer, sleeping bags, campfires. The kids were thrilled whether it was a family trip or one with the neighbours. Now their sister Sarah was going to come too. Meeting this new addition to the family was wonderful. They were all thrilled to have an older sister, and wanted to spend any time they could with her. The camping trips each summer became a tradition. Sarah came for weekend visits and we always tried to make time to be together during Easter, Christmas and Thanksgiving. Relationships grew as did an all-around love.

* * *

After Lauren had died, we took a trip that summer to Timmins to visit Mike's family. There was a birthday party for a great aunt that Mike had met once at his grandmother's funeral. This birthday party was a catalyst for a bit of a family reunion. Sarah had met a few of these extended family members at Lauren's funeral. This was an opportunity to get to know some of them a bit better, and to see the extent of her roots in Northern Ontario. As Sarah's view of her connections widened, so did her sense of family and love. She had once tried to piece together her family tree. These new roots and branches were now reaching to entwine with what she knew.

Our family honoured Lauren's life and memory by taking the trip to Australia that she had meticulously planned.. By May 2019, we were boarding a flight from Toronto to LA. This was the first leg of three that would take us to the northeastern coast of Australia. Here we would fulfil all of the dreams that Lauren had of visiting this tropical place. Together, the five of us explored and experienced this trip for Lauren.

We stayed in a gated community for two weeks in the city of

Cairns on the northeastern coast of the country. This area provided all of the excursions that Lauren had wanted to experience. The area was beautiful and lush with tropical trees and flowers everywhere. With the tropical atmosphere, we could also get a taste for the Asian influence mixed with British in the cuisine and amenities. The gated community was lovely, our accommodations a three bedroom condominium close to the pools and cafe. As we walked from the main building to our condo, I immediately noticed a decorative dragonfly on the side of one of the units. As we settled into our room, and began to explore, we felt Lauren with us as we realized the dragonfly belonged to the unit we were in.

Over the two weeks, we took boat trips to islands off the Cairns coast in the Pacific to experience coral beaches, wildlife parks, and sea turtle rescue sanctuaries. We did scuba diving at the Great Barrier Reef, and zip-lined in the RainForest. A tour bus drive up the coast provided spectacular vistas and learning about the area, its wildlife and history. An historic railway train took us into the mountain village of Kuranda where we viewed the area through the eyes of the indigenous aboriginals gaining insight on the flora and fauna of the area. A quick lesson in throwing a boomerang proved that it was an activity that required some practice.

By staying in a condominium for the two weeks, we were able to do some of our own cooking and use laundry facilities easily. Within the first week, there was a problem with the apartment sized washer so the community handyman was sent in to fix it. At the first hello, it was obvious that this gentleman wasn't native to Australia. He noticed the same of us, and of course the next communication led to us all realizing that we were from Canada. Robert, it turned out, was originally from New Brunswick. Meeting anyone from the east coast of Canada is always a thrill for me. My east coast roots still run pure through my veins and I love making connections. We became fast friends with Robert and learned about his background and how he had come to be a handyman in a gated community in Cairns Australia. We shared our tale of what brought us to Cairns, trusting our hearts to him as we told of Lauren and her wish to experience this area. As we spoke of our meaningful connection to dragonflies, the look on his face told us that this meant something to him as well. Robert, it turned out, was the one who had placed the decorative dragonfly on the outside wall of the unit that we were now in. We took this as a valid sign that this connection was supposed to happen.

Robert lived in Cairns with his girlfriend Deb, who was also from New Brunswick. They had gone to school together, and were now engaged to be married. We made arrangements to gather together for some food and conversation. This trip, though bittersweet, was a ripple of connection and love as we honoured Lauren, and pulled the fabric of our family closer together.

Each moment spent together in the pain of losing a sister, a daughter, and the joy of making memories together was a new stitch in the family fabric. We also travelled by car to New Brunswick and Nova Scotia in the late summer of 2019. Robert and Deb were getting married and we were invited to the wedding in Miramichi. The drive across the country to the east was one that we hadn't been able to do for years. Sarah had never travelled far within Canada, so she loved seeing different provinces. We took in as many sights and visits as possible. During these trips, we were all just lavishing in the fulfilment of being together. Happy that the fabric of our lives and love was holding together.

Decline - 2021

As the months after diagnosis went on each day, Sarah was drawing inward, she was sleeping more, and she wasn't getting up much. The biopsy site was draining continually, the mass growing larger.

Sarah was on a quest to use alternative methods to heal her cancer. Her attention centred on treatments she had learned about that focused on biofeedback.

This growth, however, was a monster taking over her body. To survive, her best option would be to start chemotherapy. Sarah kept many details of her diagnosis close to her chest. We wanted Sarah to know that we would help in any way that was needed. It wouldn't be hard for us to help Sarah as she went through treatments. All we could do was wait.

A Visit

By April, one year after the pandemic of 2020 had erupted across the world, people were still uneasy about visiting friends and family. The worldwide disease changed the face of our everyday interactions. I drove alone to Sarah's, prepared to be as supportive as possible. I hoped that what Sarah needed was some kindness and someone who would listen without judgement. That's what I gave her.

When I left, I felt uneasy. Sarah was relying on biofeedback treatments to shrink her breast tumour. It was very large, and required a lot of care. The two hours that we spent sitting in the backyard talking had left Sarah feeling heard. I tried to help Sarah understand the perspective of those who love her. I hoped that she would take some consideration from my experience. Sarah identified her worry about chemotherapy so I assured her that chemo was awful, but it could and often did work. When Lauren had been diagnosed and started her therapy, the lump, a collection of blasts forming in her mandible, had decreased within days. Chemo had had a hand in Lauren's ultimate death, but it wasn't what killed her. She must know that she is not an island in this. She has a family surrounding her that loves and cares about her who wants her to see this beast for what it is. Cancer waits for no one. Cancer doesn't wait idle while we decide what to do. It thrives and grows and spawns and laughs as it takes over claiming as much real estate of a body as it can. Sarah's response to this plea had been a 'but what if?'. She was comfortable with the risk. What if she was the one that beat cancer using an alternative method? What if it worked better than chemo? Wasn't it ultimately up to her?

Dilemma

An adult should be able to make their own decisions. What if a decision ultimately affects more than just that one person though? What kind of responsibility do we have or take on when we make a personal decision? When someone else's decision will directly affect my life, my well-being, do I have a right to tell them?

These thoughts and moral perplexities made pathways in my mind. Yes, it would be devastating to watch Sarah endure the inevitable outcome of her choice. It was her choice and no one else's. She was childless, no concern of leaving children without a mother. But she was a daughter, a partner, a niece, a granddaughter, and a sister. So many lives would ultimately be affected by her choice. Silently, I began to grieve for her life.

Too Much

I t was unmanageable now. Three loads of laundry a day that included sheets, towels and clothing. The pain was immeasurable, and she was losing sense of feeling in her arm.

Sarah's mother Audrey and stepfather James knew that she had to go to the hospital. Things were beyond what they could take care of at home. Sarah couldn't take it anymore. The growth was now affecting the nerves in her arm and sending pain shooting through the extremity, rendering it almost useless. She was admitted to the oncology ward at Victoria Hospital. She was now overpowered with all that this had become.

She just wanted the pain to go away. She had to succumb to the chemotherapy, and let it work. The wound created by the biopsy site and the tumour left unchecked was huge and shocking. It was unlike anything imaginable, an alien growth that once given a conduit outside the body pushed and tore through the flesh.

Comfort was found in the sway of morphine and sleep. That is all that mattered. Nothing was more meaningful. It dulled the ache. It allowed her to feel some relief. Healing was slow but steady as she allowed the forbidden chemotherapy to conquer the beast. She regained the use of her arm again. Many intravenous lines had to be used and moved over the weeks spent in hospital. While chemo had been given the opportunity to take down the formidable foe, the breast that had housed the cancerous beast had to be taken.

The final IV line became infected and the wound was quite large. It was in the left upper arm. It would require daily care even after discharge from the hospital. She hadn't completely lost her hair, but it had thinned considerably. She didn't like the way it looked. She didn't want to look like someone who was sick, who had cancer. It made it too real.

Back to Life

After a summer in the hospital, Sarah was back home at her mom's and looking forward to healing and moving forward. She wanted to reconnect and think about the next steps. She was now looking ahead, putting it all behind her. The next steps would be a plan for reconstruction of the breast. She also had to think about whether or not she wanted to have the left breast removed. Statistically, the prognosis could be better if she decided to have that done.

Slowly she was feeling like herself again. There were still moments of exhaustion; she certainly didn't have the stamina she used to. Following the pandemic, the medical system was floundering to rise above the rubble. Dates for appointments, tests and surgeries were not readily available. By late August, she had been able to spend a few weekends at her dad's, visiting her brothers, and they had come to her mom's place to stay a couple of times. It was good to reconnect with them all again. Her battle with breast cancer hadn't gone the way she had hoped, but she was still alive, so she had beaten it.

She spent the next year enjoying life. Pulling life back into herself by way of family and friends. She sought out new relationships, enjoying being as active as her body would allow her. She felt alive and triumphant, moving forward, leaving cancer behind her.

Seeing Sarah with signs of chemotherapy showing in the shape of face, gait and presence was a transportation back to Lauren's treatment. I couldn't help but be wary, as cancer had stolen my youngest daughter only four years prior. If Sarah had been fortunate enough to slip through the grasp of cancer's steely hold, it would be a cause for love and living.

One Saturday in October 2022, I felt that I should reach out to Sarah, just to let her know that I was here if needed. The message sent on that day was met with a quick reply that brought a weight of fear. Sarah responded that she was currently sitting in chairs at the Emergency Room in St. Thomas as the pain in her back was excruciating. She had been seeing a chiropractor for the last few months in hopes of getting an adjustment to end the agony. The consensus had been that one of her ribs had popped out of place, but now it was too much to take.

Painful Truth

The drive to St. Thomas was fairly quick as the highway was almost empty after midnight. Sarah had called her dad in tears following the assessment in the ER and subsequent admission to a ward. She needed some support so Mike and I bolstered ourselves with some caffeine and made our way to the hospital. Sarah hadn't eaten all day so a stop to any open eatery was necessary.

The emergency room physician was there immediately with a voice and demeanour that spoke volumes. While Sarah was struggling to take in all of the painful truth, we knew that the situation was dire. The doctor explained that many lesions and spots were visible on Sarah's liver and possibly her bones, indicating that the triple negative breast cancer had metastasized. She indicated that this was a very sad diagnosis, but said that there would be next steps that included a transfer to Victoria Hospital in London for further tests, biopsy and plan of action for chemotherapy. At the very most, this would provide some more time. Time, which Sarah was now limited to.

We stayed with Sarah for a couple of hours until she felt a bit more settled. I confided that the worst news was what I suspected when Sarah had told me she had been experiencing enough pain to go to the ER.

When Lauren had died, it had been a very acute and ferocious illness and end. Sepsis had taken hold with a quiet and calculating sharpness that left them all in shock. Now we were faced with the death of another daughter. The doctor at St. Thomas General had said 'I'm so sorry' multiple times. Sorry. Her words were ringing in my ears. When a health professional says sorry it usually means that the situation is critical.

Tearing

The tearing of fabric was almost audible as we drove back to Cambridge. It was still dark. We had travelled to St. Thomas and back in the middle of the night. Hearing the news and sitting with Sarah, trying to make sense of the reality and harshness of it all. From that night onward we felt as though every step we took was underwater. Each moment muffled and echoing in our souls. Our souls screaming for light and love and comfort, knowing that our hearts were ripping apart again.

As October lumbered into November, there were pieces coming together. We waited and hoped to hear how things were progressing, confused by the seeming lack of urgency following such a heart-wrenching prognosis. I was getting some updates from Sarah, but it just didn't seem to be fitting together right. The weight of it all in October was palpable, but now she was home, and nothing was being done as far as treatment.

Broken

The tests that were all supposed to happen the next day had been drawn out over a month and more. The pain Sarah was feeling was horrific. Thankfully she had a small supply of pain medication from before, but they were proving to be less and less effective. Calls to oncologists and pain specialists were dead ends as answering systems were bogged down. Some test results began to filter in by the end of the month, showing that there were no lesions interfering with her skeletal system, and blood work looked normal. Her liver function didn't show any signs of dysfunction, but the size of her abdomen was concerning. There was still no plan in place. Sarah was getting all of these tests done as an out-patient, and had yet to be seen by an oncologist. The doctor in emergency back in October had definitely made it sound as though her case, due to the seriousness, would be expedited. Now, after a month, it seemed as though things were not as bad. Physical symptoms, however, told a different story. Sarah began to get fevers of unknown origin, which brought her once again to the emergency department in St. Thomas. Here she was admitted, and blood work showed that she was anaemic and would need a blood transfusion. After a month of trying to get tests and biopsies done, and get more information on her condition to no avail, an oncologist arrived in Sarah's room to tell her the news. The tumour in her liver was now the size of a football. No course of therapy or surgery could help. There was nothing left to do.

There was no denying the feeling. Broken. Shock. Despite her efforts it had come back. This had to be a mistake. They were leaving her to die, and it wasn't right. Sarah was in shock, and couldn't believe that this was happening. She had no idea that the pain she had been dealing with since August would be related to her breast cancer. She had beaten that. She was finally getting her life back. She had gone back to work on a modified week. She allowed herself to feel victorious. She wouldn't let this happen. She had gone out and bought a new car. She was going to outlive this. They were wrong.

People started to visit. They were coming over to see her, as though it would be the last time. She felt as though everyone was writing her off. She didn't want to hear anyone talk about it. It was just too much to process. She was settled in at her mom's. Back in her comfortable bed. She didn't want it to be true.

The News

Two to four months. A thirty-four year old woman would be dead in two to four months because of cancer. It was a story that was told frequently to anyone who would listen. The colour pink screamed it each fall as women donned the colour to walk, run and raise awareness of the beast. The honouring was there for anyone who had battled and survived, or anyone who held a woman who had succumbed despite their battle, in their hearts. Now Sarah would be one of those women. It was unfathomable, yet… not unexpected. The dread we had felt, the truth we didn't want to believe was now being laid out before us.

After a month of hearing that most tests were looking positive, it was a shock to receive the message from Sarah that there was nothing that could be done, and that she had months to live. We drove to Aylmer to see Sarah. It was the day before Theo's birthday. There was a tear as the fabric weakened under the strain.

The tumour had grown significantly over the month. We sat around the table in Audrey and James's home. Two couples who held a common love for Sarah. The conversation was full of logic and reality. The prognosis had been clear.

* * *

Through it all, the splinters that broke through the pain; were memories. The trigger could be a mere stray thought, or a smell. Definitely a photo could take her back. She was tired, and just wanted to rest. The pain was there too. It jabbed at her, pulling her out of the bliss of medicated sleep. She would need more drugs to send it away again. The pain and nausea needed to be quelled.

Sarah's mind would drift to a time when she had dreams. Dreams of a home and a family. She was calculated and discerning when it came to personal relationships. She didn't take love lightly. It was important to her that she find the right person to spend the rest of her life with. A home, together with the person you love. Her person. Had he been the right one though? The pain she had endured during their breakup had been immense. In the beginning, the love they shared seemed unconquerable. Then her illness had taken over.

Relationships can be broken by a single thread. When looking through the lens that love uses to draw you in, your heart and your mind may not be ready to withstand life's cruel twists and turns. Is it love when someone walks away from the relationship because of differing views? Was it really the deep and lasting love that would carry two hearts through the depths and heights of life? Sarah wanted to believe that this love that she felt, the love that had grown, was the kind that would last. Then it had all fallen apart. The struggle of her health and decisions on treatment had been too much weight for the relationship to withstand.

The pain that the shattering of this relationship had caused was deep and scarring. The pain itself was like a cancer that she needed to cut loose from her being. Her world was imploding around her. She had only her family to help her pick up the pieces. When she was barely able to move they were there, helping her.

These memories were not the ones that she wanted to hold with her now. Her mind needed to take her to happier times. She didn't want to die. She didn't want this to be the end.

Pray For a Miracle

November gave way into December, but not before there was a glimmer of hope. The hope was to provide Sarah with some comfort and some time. The prognosis was the same. Sarah hoped for more than that. The oncologists only offered an olive branch. She would try chemotherapy. If there was any sign that her liver was getting worse with the treatment they would have to stop. Everyone prayed that the result would be positive, that the tumour would show signs of shrinking. Instead, it was called off. The result was elevated numbers indicating that her liver couldn't withstand the treatment. It was just a week before Christmas.

The Hail Mary approach was put into motion. There was a determination that more could be done despite the ominous death sentence that had been bestowed. The system had failed her, and now it was time that someone knew it and that something be done about it. Phone calls were made and letters were written. Sarah's general practitioner was shocked to learn of her condition. He had not received anything from an oncologist since October. Before she went to see her GP, Sarah had travelled to Princess Margaret Cancer Centre in Toronto in the hopes that they would take her in. Would this hospital accept a patient without a referral? It was hard to fathom. We waited through the day for some news. Finally, a call and request to stop in to rest.

Sarah was exhausted. I guided her to a bedroom where she could rest while we caught up on the news from the hospital. They had been very kind, and resourceful. While they couldn't take Sarah in without a referral, they explained the process and wished them the best. They gave Audrey tips on who to connect with and how to ensure the referral was seen and reviewed with expedition.

Maybe this was something. Maybe this renowned hospital would have a therapy that would be proven helpful. Dr. Carter, the GP, prepared a referral. It was just days before Christmas, so we knew the weekends and holidays would affect how quickly they would get an answer.

Letting Go

She was dying. My stepdaughter was dying and I wanted to help. I reflected and contemplated the weight of it all. It wasn't Sarah's job to make me feel better about her dying. I wanted Sarah to be able to die the way she chose. Was she even making decisions about that? Did she know how she wanted to die? My fear was that when her reality forced its way in, lucidity would merely be a fringe on the fabric of her being. I let Sarah know that we would be there when she needed us. And then we waited.

Just after the new year had been rung in, Sarah had been granted a room at Parkwood Hospital in palliative care.

* * *

Try to imagine what it would be like to be told that you had months to live. Can you? Can your mind wrap itself around that possibility and then come out whole and ready? Who's to say how someone, anyone should take that news. How they should act, what they should do. Acceptance, denial, fight, flight, retreat. Sleep. Pain, medicate, sleep. Nausea, pain, medicate sleep. Now, people say they love you. People want to come and see you. It was even difficult to think. The fog was heavier now.

* * *

Like a whisper it was her last breath. She knew it was coming. She had given up trying to deny it. If she had regrets, only she would know. It was an exhausting struggle. She was back in that room. There were nurses and doctors there. It was their job to make sure she was comfortable and pain-free. She had only wanted to sleep. Through the fog she thought she could hear their voices. The ones who came to tell her they loved her. The ones who came to tell her to fight. Her body wouldn't let her respond. All she could do was listen. Listen and breathe, but even that was harder now. Her body was letting the cancer take over. Each breath felt like an eternity. There was a light, and there was love and she did it. She took one last breath.

Special Memories

Sarah was a very caring, loving, outgoing person with a love of sports and artwork. She will be missed immensely by so many people who touched her life as well as her special cat Keira. Sarah was an inspired, award-winning artist. She had an eye for colours and a talent with the brush that is seen in the pieces that were created by her hand. She attended Arthur Voaden Secondary School, King's College, and Western University. She worked in the intake office at Western University.

Sarah enjoyed volunteering at Support Services (LifeSpin), Middlesex Victim Services and as a Crisis Intervention respondent. She was kind and a good friend to many. Sarah was determined and willful, with a sprinkle of stubbornness to spice things up. When it came to decision-making, she was calculating, discerning and bright, taking time to weigh all sides. A fun-loving person, Sarah enjoyed spending time with friends whether it was golfing, playing volleyball, movie watching or gaming. She had a great sense of humour and loved to laugh. Sarah enjoyed singing, but saved this special talent for select ears. She was once overheard saying that singing the right song could be the real emotional release that one might need in certain situations.

Sarah was our bold, beautiful and girl, loved by her mother, her stepfather, her father, her stepmother, grandparents, uncles, cousins and many friends. Her smile was infectious, her eyes sparkled and she wore these natural assets with confidence.

* * *

I miss the conversations we would have. She was learning to use her intuitive gift. She loved to read and learn about spirituality, using the knowledge to discover herself and find her own unique path. What I will miss the most are the moments when we were all together as a family. Sarah was enjoying her brothers and sister. They were bonding and becoming friends. There was a time that I felt this love for each other would endure anything.

Part 3

The Dark and the Light
— A Parent's Grief
The ramblings and the writings

Numb

I believe I have become numb to the heartache and pain. I have numbed myself as a means of protection. Reading about hospital stays seems like an everyday occurrence now. Most every connection in my life weaves its way to grief, loss, sickness.

If I peel back that layer of protection, I am raw and exposed. Unable to function. A mass of tears, worry, dread, defeat...

You know you must focus on the positive in order to get through each day, hour, and minute. You put aside your deepest fears so that life can go on. You try to bounce back, all the while knowing that the threat of illness lurks.

Each day, each moment, is a gift. No matter how trivial.

There is very little grace given to those who do not know. I want you to know but at the same time, I don't want you to have to understand. I want to scream at you, a stranger, "Ask me! Ask me about my family. Ask me about my children." I want to talk about them. I want you to know.

As grief is so very personal and unique to each person who must walk its path, others, those who have not had to experience this particular type of grief, either won't know what to say, or won't say the right thing, as there is really no right thing. Perhaps the right thing to say is nothing. Say that you will be there to listen. Say that you want to listen, say that you will sit and use your ears, you will ask questions, you will offer a shoulder, a hug and a tear. Then you stop. Don't talk. There's nothing to say. Just listen if only to the silence of my pain.

My grief has travelled a path not unlike one provided by a rollercoaster. During the five years since Lauren has died, and now with the death of Sarah, I have noticed that there is not much goodwill given to those who attempt to do or say something to help or provide comfort. Each will try to provide comfort within the realm of their own perspective. This may not fit into my personal needs. Their efforts may seem to be callous and unfeeling. Their attempts met with shudders and shock. It seems that those outside who try to help are well meaning. I give them grace, and accept the comfort as it was intended, not how it might affect. My grief is my own and I must wear it, whether under a mask or not. There are days that I don my mask of normalcy to help me get through the hours until I can hide inside myself again. Other days, that mask slips away, showing the rawness beneath. The shell I have become.

* * *

As I look around me, I see so much pain, and sorrow mixed with the joy. I know life is good. Life is also a crashing of moments that aren't what we hope for. Is it right for me to say that we were 'thrust into this world of childhood cancer'? Our beautiful girl is no longer a physical presence on this earth due to this 'world.' Were we 'thrust into the world of organ donation' or the 'world of endocrine disease'?

What I have come to realize is that we were never 'thrust' anywhere. It has always been here. If we didn't see it we just mindlessly chose to turn away.

I'm not saying we shouldn't find joy in anything. Of course we should. I just struggle to find the balance. The sense. How does it make sense that beautiful families are once again facing years of treatment as their child's cancer has returned? How does it make sense that children are in hospitals waiting for life-saving organs? A wait that is incredibly long, difficult, and so unbearably unknown. How does any of this make sense? How do I find joy in this?

The joy is in the love. The bittersweet love that fills my heart and soul with each memory of Lauren▨

The love that I have for every child I've met on this journey. The pain and deep sorrow I feel bubbles to the surface as I try to let the love remind me that life can be good in the midst of all of this.

Each day that I awaken to know that I have 2 boys, who have become young men, reminds me that there is joy. Every connection that I have made with any parent over the last 21 years of this life has given me pause to know joy and love in this place we call life.

My family has grown to include so many who are together and find love due to circumstance.

So. In all of this, I say, find joy in every moment. If you are blessed to have never known the pain and anguish of watching your child go through unspeakable suffering due to illness, treatments, medications, surgeries... then you have much to be grateful for.

Please remember each day that you are extremely blessed. Please remember each day that we are all struggling in some way. It may not be apparent, but we are. Give grace. Have patience. Show kindness and love. Find joy. Send positive thoughts to those who are struggling.

* * *

And I would live every moment of our life over again just to see you. This wave of grief is so deep and harsh and raw. I feel as though I cannot move or think. The emptiness I feel is so overwhelming. I know, I do know that you are around me. I know that you are here. But today at this moment I don't want to go on without you. I am struggling to understand how someone so beautiful could be taken away; in such a harsh and awful way. I relive your last days as a movie in my mind, over and over again.

* * *

Say her name. Say it with the feeling that you keep in your heart having known her. Say it. Lauren. Say it knowing that though it may seem to cause us sadness. The sadness will always be there. Say her name without fear, for hearing her name may bring tears, but also joy to know she will never be forgotten. She remains in our hearts and our actions. She taught me to have grace and courage. She teaches me to love and to give.

I recently read an article stating scientific evidence that a child's DNA passes to its mother before birth, the mother therefore always having a part of that child within them.

Each day I miss Lauren with every piece of my being. Yet I go on, with her pushing me to be the best I can be.

* * *

As I reflect on the moments that crowd my brain, the missing is the hardest part. There will always be pain as I miss sweet Lauren Rose. There will always be love too. For love is what carries me through each day. There's a peace that is hard to describe. I feel her with me, yet know she is gone.

So now, on a day that marks what would have been her 17th birthday, I feel pain and love, peace and longing.

* * *

Feeling

Screaming in the shower. Crying because your heart has been ripped apart. Two sisters, souls forever entwined. When Sarah was diagnosed with breast cancer, I felt her slipping away then. I was already unconsciously mourning her death. I wanted to be positive for her. I wanted to believe that despite it all she would survive. My heart knew otherwise. Sarah was an adult. Still a daughter, but not a child. An adult. She had every right to live her life the way she chose. She had the right to make her own decisions despite the outcome. Was that her soul's lesson? The pain created through her choice is what I live with. I struggle now to find my soul's lesson in this loss. The pain and loss endured over the years often holds me like a vice. I worry about the effects of it all on my husband and my sons. If I let it all take over I worry that there would be nothing left of me. I have to work each day to keep that from happening. The deep dark pit of despair beckons quietly. It would be easier to lie down and let it envelope me as I find myself lost in the mundane pace of what everyday life has become. I need and want more than what I see in front of me. I do not feel that this is all there is. If nothing else, the pain and loss have taken me on a journey that lays open before me. It is up to me, each day, to choose whether or not I will take a step down the path of enlightenment to a world that is far beyond this earth. Strange to think that the loss of lives; that grief; would be the conduit to learning about a deeper connection to life. Or is it? Isn't it the death of someone who we love that inevitably leads us to ponder life itself, our own 'raison d'etre'?

Each day I wish that I were closer to seeing these two bright souls again. Each day I am closer. Closer than the day before. I search for signs that they are with me. I search for the lessons that I believe I am here to experience with each moment of my existence. I search for my true self, trying to feel my way as I find out who I am meant to be.

I could squelch through the emotions of my grief as it is served to me each day, allowing it to take its hold on me. A deep need wants to allow it. A concerted effort is made each day to take the fingers that grip and hold me down; peel them back and let them fall away into the deepest part of myself only to crawl out and grasp me back again at the end of each day. When I release their grasp, I take hold of what pieces of me are left and strive to be the best me that I can muster. Trying to become — what? I am still learning. What I know is that my soul is searching, my heart is aching, and I'm still here. Feeling all of it. Still standing. Somehow. A question which I often take as a rhetorical one. 'How are you still standing?'

The Ripples Continue

L auren and Sarah, now together, sisters. I wish so much that their lives had been different. That they could have experienced more on this earthly plane. I sit and listen to my fellow bereaved parents. We know each other by heart. Each of our stories is as unique as the children whom we grieve for. Does anyone ever look ahead when they are sitting, dreaming, wondering what their life will be like; imagining that their life will be a ripple of trauma and loss? Do they feel it in their bones? Did I?

Each of the lives of my children have impacted who I am. Each of their stories ripple in my being. An odd thing happened in 2021. A freak accident that brought about the loss of a finger for my son Zach. During the long recovery of the initial injury, he began to notice that each of his fingernails had ripples in them. These ripples started at the base, and throughout the recovery and subsequent amputation of his finger, they moved along his nails until they came to the end of his nails. His body reacting to the trauma. Ripples extending outward. This is what each beautiful and heart-breaking connection has done to me. Each life, each being, each connection a ripple reverberating through my body slowly changing me to be who I am meant to be. Becoming me. Always and forever.

* * *

Their whole life ahead of them, all the good and all the bad,
the triumphs and mistakes, gone like a story erased.
~Raymond Reddington - The Blacklist S7 E15

DEATH

is the greatest teacher of all.
Greater than all human philosophies.
Truer than any religion.
Death strips away the lies, the pretence.
Death makes a mockery of our resentment.
It burns our greed, grudges and grievances.
Death invites us to be utterly present.
To let go.
To forgive.
To meet, without history.
Death makes it plain that only love matters.
That only love makes life worth living.
And all else is dust.
Death is a ruthless portal.
Worldly riches are powerless against it.
Hatred cannot survive it.
Only love can pass through it.
We return to our True Nature.
The cycle is complete.

- Jeff Foster

There is a sacredness in tears.
They are not the mark of weakness but of power.
They are messengers of overwhelming grief
and of unspeakable love.
~Washington Irving

When tears flow like rain. All of the love I feel. All of that love bursting in the essence of my being, with nowhere to go.

When it rains now, I am transported to simpler times. Life before the trauma, the loss, the grief. I want to run, but instead, I sit and let the rain pour over me — as do the memories of all the love we built. I watch as the ripples form in the puddles. Connecting, and affecting. Life.

* * *

She left us like a crash in the night that startles and shakes you longer than it should.

I let my broken heart be all that I was.

Epilogue

I don't want to know you.

I see you. You say you will get to know me, that we become all too familiar to one another. I don't want to know you. You are the first face we see when we enter.

I don't want to know you.

I see you. You look like me. You're a mom. You smile through your worry. Your child feels like crap as they curl themselves into a ball on the chair covered by a warm blanket. The IV beeps and they stir slightly. I don't want to know you.

I see you. You're a young child. Your hair grows back sporadically. You play at the train table and laugh. You look for your dad and run in for a hug. I don't want to know you.

I don't want to know you. You are the compassion, and brain. You are the words of statistics, the words of knowledge and comfort. The words of unbearable news that we must bear. We live by your guidance and your words. We must believe. I don't want to know you.

I see you. You sleep in a chair curled up beside your child as their chemo infusion drips silently into their body through the IV tube. You know that the drive home may be difficult. You want to get your child home safely so they can rest. You rest now, as you know rest may not be possible later. I don't want to know you.

I see you. I see your eyes. Red rimmed from tears and worry. Another fever. Another admission. Days away from home and family. I don't want to know you.

I hear you. I hear you scream as the nurses try to put a needle into your port. Again. It's the last thing you want. It's something you need. They tell you that you have to stay. You are not going home today like you had hoped. You want your home. You just want to be a child. I don't want to know you.

I see you. You smile, you laugh, you race with your child through the hallways of the hospital. You fill your days with medicine, needles, feeding apparatus, and as much fun as you can muster. Your child needs this. You need this. I see you. I don't want to know you.

I see you. The fight has been long and exhausting. I don't want to know you. You want the fight to end, but it must end with a victory. You weep in the shower. You weep by yourself. You cling to hope. You cling to the words of the professionals. I don't want to know you.

I see you. You see the light. You see the end of the journey. It is so close. It is close yet it is still just outside the grasp of your tired and battered reach. I don't want to know you.

I hear you. You whisper comforting words. Your beloved child wretches again. You wipe their mouth and their brow. I don't want to know you. ...but I do.

I do know you. I know the light and the bones of you. You are every person we have seen and met since this journey started. I know you and I love you. You are within me now. A part of me that I never wanted to know. A part of me that I would gladly expel if I could. If only I could open my mouth and scream you out. A scream so loud that it would deafen all of those who don't know. I would scream it all out. All out so that all could hear. I would scream it out to have her back.

I don't want to know you, but I do. I love you. I love you all. I will never forget you, as you are a part of me that I never wanted to be, but I am.

I am a mom who grieves for two daughters because of cancer.

Acknowledgments

Thank you to my husband for being forgiving and loving. Thank you to Theo, Zach and Lauren for giving me the gift of being your mother. Sarah, thank you for accepting me as your stepmom. As each situation is unique, you are always and forever an important and meaningful member of our family.

My good friends. You know who you are. You stayed with me. You listened. You were there when I needed you. I wouldn't be here without your support and encouragement.

Go Gold families. We were beside each other through some of the worst times of our lives. You are forever family.

Compassionate Friends parents. The worst possible pain in our lives brought us together. Knowing you are there for support helped me with each word I wrote.

Your lives have affected me profoundly.

Mark. I don't know where I'd be if it weren't for your gift. You have opened my heart and my mind, connected me to my sweet Lauren in a way that I needed. Bless you.

Sarah, you brought a new joy into our lives. Your connection with us was growing and evolving and then you were gone. We love you and we miss you.

Lauren, you are my light. You provided messages through Mark that I should write the story. So I did.

Notes

James Neil Hollingworth *(1933–1996) was a beatnik, hippie, writer, and former manager of the psychedelic folk rock bands Quicksilver Messenger Service and Ace of Cups. He wrote under the pseudonym Ambrose Hollingworth Redmoon. [wikipedia]*

Pluviophile - (n) a lover of rain; someone who finds joy and peace of mind during rainy days.